Gilligan's Island

TV Milestones

Series Editors
Barry Keith Grant
Brock University

Jeannette Sloniowski
Brock University

TV Milestones is part of the Contemporary Approaches to Film and Media Series

A complete listing of the books in this series can be found online at wsupress.wayne.edu

General Editor
Barry Keith Grant
Brock University

Advisory Editors
Robert J. Burgoyne
University of St. Andrews

Tom Gunning
University of Chicago

Caren J. Deming
University of Arizona

Thomas Leitch
University of Delaware

Patricia B. Erens
School of the Art Institute of Chicago

Anna McCarthy
New York University

Peter X. Feng
University of Delaware

Walter Metz
Southern Illinois University

Lucy Fischer
University of Pittsburgh

Lisa Parks
University of California–
Santa Barbara

Frances Gateward
Ursinus College

GILLIGAN'S ISLAND

Walter C. Metz

TV MILESTONES SERIES

Wayne State University Press Detroit

16 15 14 13 12   5 4 3 2 1

Library of Congress Cataloging-in-Publication Data

Metz, Walter, 1967–
Gilligan's Island / Walter C. Metz.
p. cm. — (TV milestones)
Includes bibliographical references and index.
ISBN 978-0-8143-3372-3 (pbk. : alk. paper) — ISBN 978-0-8143-3647-2 (e-book)
1. Gilligan's Island (Television program) I. Title.
PN1992.77.G53M47 2012
791.45′72—dc23
2011030712

∞

CONTENTS

ACKNOWLEDGMENTS

This book is dedicated to my three children, Alex, Emma, and
Charlie. They were the willing subjects of my crazy research
experiment to see if they would love *Gilligan's Island* as much as
I do. I am delighted to report that, despite being taken off the
air, the allure of this deceptively simple show continues to hold
the next generation spellbound, now through DVDs instead of
broadcast airings. Much of this book's content is inspired by
their astute observations about their favorite episodes. In particular, Charlie's obsession with "Pass the Vegetables, Please" led
me to write my favorite section of this book, on the Bakhtinian, carnivalesque dimensions of *Gilligan's Island*. I find it awe-
inspiring, and encouraging for the future, that a little boy's endless rewatching of an episode could teach me so much about
the media landscape that I have scrutinized with adult eyes for
twenty years.

I, of course, owe tremendous debts, both personal and
professional, to far too many people to enumerate here. Most
important, my wife, Anneke, continues to inspire my creativity and put up with the drudgery of being married to a neu-
rotic writer. My new colleagues at Southern Illinois University,
through their kind collegiality, have renewed my enthusiasm

for an academic administrative career. One of them, Sue Felleman, kindly led me toward Lynn Spigel's work on television and art history, which solved one of the many blocks I was having in finishing this book.

Finally, I owe many thanks to my students, who have endured endless lecture digressions about *Gilligan's Island* in courses as far ranging as those on the American West in the nineteenth century and the theater of ancient Greece. I have learned a tremendous amount about *Gilligan's Island* from my students at the University of Texas at Austin, Montana State University, the Free University Berlin, and Southern Illinois University.

Acknowledgments

Introduction:
A Minimalist Allegory

At the end of the episode "Gilligan Goes Gung-Ho" (season 3, episode 83, December 26, 1966), the *Gilligan's Island* castaways decide they need a police force. Due to the duplicitous machinations of the other petty, self-promoting male castaways (the Skipper [Alan Hale Jr.], Mr. Howell [Jim Backus], and the Professor [Russell Johnson]), young Gilligan (Bob Denver) is elected deputy. At first, the boy rises to the task, but by mid-episode, he is unable to distinguish between minor infractions and major transgressions. Gilligan locks all six of his compatriots (the men as well as Ginger [Tina Louise], Mary Ann [Dawn Wells], and Mrs. Howell [Natalie Schafer]) in a cave with bamboo bars serving as a jail. As the episode continues, the castaways attempt to trick Gilligan in an escape plot but only succeed in luring the lad into the cave himself, after which he throws away the key, trapping them all inside. Fatefully, an airplane flies over the island at this exact moment. Because they are all locked in the cave, none of the islanders are able to light their SOS signal made from wooden logs. As a consequence, not of anarchy, but of law and order—that is, the imposition of hierarchical civilization on the natural order of the island—the castaways are once again forced to live in exile for at least another week.

This episode is emblematic of the cultural importance of *Gilligan's Island* (CBS, 1964–67). While typically reviled for its episodic inanity—stupid Gilligan yet again keeps the castaways from being rescued—it is my contention that this narrative minimalism (how many times can Gilligan do something stupid to keep those poor people from getting rescued?) is the source of the show's startling invention. Instead of imbecility, the show produces a vibrant critique of dominant American values. The repetition encourages the posing of a very different question: *Why* would the castaways want to be rescued when they in fact live in a utopia far away from the dysfunctions of mainland America? Or, as Laura Morowitz puts it in her study of the episode "Goodbye, Old Paint" (season 1, episode 34, May 22, 1965) in which a Paul Gauguin–like primitivist painter depicts Ginger as a Balinese dancer:

> The hope of rescue raises another essential meta-theme of the series: the castaways' constant desire to return to Western civilization. We might well wonder why the castaways would want to leave the island; material abundance, companionship, and an absence of the stresses and dangers of "civilized" life render Gilligan's island a tropical paradise. Yet the castaways are forever in search of a way "home." The reality of elsewhere can never match the dream, as Gauguin knew all too well. . . . As postindustrial Westerners, they cannot remain in the realm of the timeless and ahistorical (a realm reserved only for "natives"). Movement is a prerequisite of their condition. . . . Capitalism always seeks an elsewhere. (122)

Morowitz forwards a way of thinking about not the simplicity but the complexity of *Gilligan's Island*. The issue is not so much about how repetitive the episodes are but what interest that repetition produces. The contradiction of the show is that its long-term narrative obsesses about rescue, whereas the themes of its individual episodes scream out an intense regard for the island's utopian isolation from a corrupt mainland civilization. Not only is this *Gilligan's Island*'s central motif, as Morowitz observes, but television's itself. Lucy Ricardo (Lucille Ball) on *I Love Lucy* (CBS, 1950–59) is stuck on her island, an apartment in Manhattan where she can never break into Ricky's show; Frank Furillo (Daniel J. Travanti) on *Hill St. Blues* (NBC, 1981–87) fights a crime-riddled city from his island office in the midst of an overburdened police precinct; and Jerry on *Seinfeld* (NBC, 1990–98) is confined to his apartment like a Samuel Beckett prison, as the finale of that series makes quite explicit. All television allegorizes the isolating nature of American "island" life and our communal attempts to overcome its consequences; *Gilligan's Island* is simply the most explicit show in the history of the medium concerning these circumstances.

Over the course of many years, I came to fall in love with the seven castaways on *Gilligan's Island* as a special experiential part of my love of television itself. Seeing the islanders in syndication each weekday afternoon after school became a refuge from the troubles of real life. Coming into our homes with familiar characters who, if a show is successful, visit us for many years, television provides the possibility of coming to live with fictional characters on a symbolic island utopia. Whether Morowitz is correct or not in arguing that the contradiction of *Gilligan's Island* is reducible to capitalism's foibles is one of the projects of this book. Drawing from Morowitz's and similar insights into the cultural possibilities engaged by the show, this book offers a passionate defense of *Gilligan's Island,* a seemingly idiotic 1960s telefilm sitcom, from a perspective emphasizing the narrative and social productivity of its obvious minimalism.

The Existential Island

By placing seven stereotypical characters on an isolated island, the show's creator, Sherwood Schwartz, is able to engage in absurdist comedy that interrogates without distraction basic questions of human behavior. As such, the show's primary intertext is, unexpectedly, Samuel Beckett's *Waiting for Godot* (1953), a play in which two characters stand on a stage waiting to be "rescued" by Godot, and yet he never arrives. Similarly, the seven castaways on the island try to get rescued for ninety-eight episodes only to be forever stranded in the South Pacific when the show was canceled by William Paley's wife, Babe, who enjoyed *Gunsmoke* (CBS, 1955–75), even though that western series was, by 1967, poorly rated and equally exhausted of new ideas,

Dodge City being just one more 1960s televisual island (Stod-dard 306).

Even the afterlife of *Gilligan's Island* testifies to its radical en-dorsement of perpetual stasis: in the three made-for-TV movies released years after the cancellation of the show—*Rescue from Gilligan's Island* (1978), *The Castaways on Gilligan's Island* (1979), and *The Harlem Globetrotters on Gilligan's Island* (1981)—the castaways almost immediately return to the island from which they purportedly were so desperate to escape. At the end of *Res-cue from Gilligan's Island,* the castaways find mainland America so corrupt that they take another cruise to escape and are once again shipwrecked on their old island. In *Castaways,* they run a hotel to share the joys of their island with others. For their part, Vladimir and Estragon in Beckett's play end each day deciding enthusiastically to leave their plot of land, but each time the stage directions indicate "they do not move" as the lights go down to end the act.

Furthermore, *Waiting for Godot* offers a testament to the transformative power of love: Vladimir and Estragon while away the time by telling jokes, being mean to each other, fight-ing, just talking. In short, they love each other as if they are married. Similarly, the seven castaways love one another: they feud, they scheme in petty ways (Who is the most beautiful woman on the island? or, Who should be president?), but they continue caring about one another week after week, which, as Nel Noddings suggests, is a central aspect of radical feminism.

I have dedicated my career to mining the similarities in the humanist caring and intellectual merits of high and low culture; in Sherwood Schwartz—the much-maligned creator and exec-utive producer of *Gilligan's Island* and *The Brady Bunch* (ABC, 1969–74)—I find the great televisual auteur of such values. Schwartz began his career studying biology in Southern Cali-fornia. After he began successfully writing jokes for Bob Hope's radio show, he built a new career in television comedy writing for such shows as *The Adventures of Ozzie and Harriet* (ABC,

1952–66) and *The Red Skelton Show* (NBC/CBS, 1951–71). After supervising the scripts for *My Favorite Martian* (CBS, 1963–66), Schwartz got his pilot for *Gilligan's Island* picked up by CBS for the 1964 fall season. In pitching *Gilligan's Island* to William Paley at the CBS television network, he argued for the show as "a social microcosm." After he was rejected as an egghead intellectual, he returned with the famous theme song—"Just sit right back / And you'll hear a tale / A tale of a fateful trip, / That started from a tropic port, / Aboard this tiny ship"—which he performed for the network executives. The pilot was ordered for production. The housing of *Gilligan's Island* in simplicity—the catchy theme song, the slapstick comedy, and the simplistic plots (Gilligan once again foils the rescue attempts of the other castaways)—masks its tremendous achievement as a humanist testament to the ability of human beings to love one another in the tradition of the great works of Western civilization; the analysis of that intertextual web is the purpose of this book.

One of the important modernist themes grappled with by *Gilligan's Island* is the crisis of communication. As Vladimir and Estragon stand on the stage, they allegorize the difficulties human beings have in communicating with one another. Indeed, most episodes of *Gilligan's Island* revolve around miscommunications that require the castaways to invent strategies, many involving performance, to close the gap of understanding between the characters. For example, in "Where There's a Will" (season 3, episode 74, October 17, 1966), after making out his will, Mr. Howell comes to believe that his fellow castaways are trying to murder him for the inheritance money. He stumbles upon the Skipper sharpening his machete to "slaughter the old boar," meaning an actual pig, not Mr. Howell. However, when the castaways believe Mr. Howell has disappeared in quicksand and died, he hears their earnest sorrow. The Skipper declares, "He was one of us. I feel that I've lost a brother." Schwartz uses his medium to declare that, with love, miscommunications can be resolved in as little as twenty-three minutes.

However, other episodes of *Gilligan's Island* engage the modern dynamics of communication more directly and aggressively, as Beckett himself did in plays such as *Krapp's Last Tape* (1958) in which an old man listens to recordings he made as a young man, desperately trying to wring meaning out of the audio technology's products. In "You've Been Disconnected" (season 2, episode 53, November 13, 1966), Schwartz's show most directly grapples with the crisis that modern technologies pose for human communication. The radio is a vexing object on *Gilligan's Island*. It communicates information to the castaways, more often than not to torment them, without helping them to get rescued. Indeed, comically, the radio announcer can seem to hear the castaways, responding to them directly without ever completing the circuit and asking them for their location. For example, in "The Sweepstakes" (season 1, episode 42, October 14, 1965), when the radio announces that Gilligan holds the winning ticket in a lottery, Gilligan says that it cannot be true. The radio announcer assures Gilligan that it is really the case that his ticket has the correct winning number.

In "You've Been Disconnected," however, the radio's communications problems are compounded telephonically. After a terrible storm, Gilligan discovers that the transpacific communications cable has washed up in the lagoon. After difficulties breaking the hard casing to access the telephone lines, the Professor finally opens the cable and assigns the castaways to monitor the lines. Again, communication proves a one-way affair. The Skipper learns that a Hawaiian gang is getting ready to rob a bank, but can do little about it. Indeed, this replicates the plot of Grand Guignol turn-of-the-century melodramas, such as André De Lorde's play, *Au Téléphone* (1902), which ends with a husband listening to his wife on the phone as she is strangled to death by a murderer with the phone cord itself. The husband impotently listens, unable to intervene across the physical distance. Back on the island, Gilligan finally reaches an operator in San Diego. However, she demands that he insert an additional dime into the pay phone. When he cannot do so, she hangs up on him. Another storm washes the cable out to sea before the castaways can establish any meaningful telephonic communication with the mainland. Quite simply, as in a Grand Guignol melodrama, modern technology is just as incompetent as Gilligan in getting the castaways rescued.

In one of the most beloved episodes of the series, "Smile, You're on Mars Camera" (season 2, episode 40, October 7, 1965), the castaways confront the failure of *visual* communication technology. A NASA Mars probe crash-lands on the island. After much hilarity chasing after the probe's lens, the Professor finally gets the camera functioning. However, the combination of Gilligan's bird feather collection and the Professor's glue for securing the lens proves deadly to the castaways' rescue

The Professor taps into the transpacific telephone cable in "You've Been Disconnected" (January 13, 1966).

attempts when subjected to Gilligan's shenanigans. Thinking that their spacecraft has actually landed on Mars, the NASA scientists activate the camera at precisely the moment Gilligan explodes the Professor's glue pot amid his pile of bird feathers, covering the castaways. The festooned islanders strut in front of the camera, attempting to get NASA to come rescue them. However, NASA believes that Mars's inhabitants must be "chicken people." Before the castaways can clean themselves up, Gilligan trips over the probe, destroying the lens for good this time. Thus, in these and other ways, *Gilligan's Island* reveals the comic nature of the failure of human communication, especially when purportedly assisted by technology, resulting in yet another failure at getting rescued from the island.

8

The castaways as chicken people in "Smile, You're on Mars Camera" (October 7, 1965).

A Boy and His Whale

In his book about the creation of the show, *Inside* Gilligan's Island, Schwartz claims his intention was to demonstrate to postwar America how people of varying backgrounds needed to get along to survive as an allegory for Cold War America. Given the success of the program—globally, the most successfully syndicated show in television history—it seems likely that he succeeded. Yet, from an academic perspective, *Gilligan's Island*'s success at making people care about one another needs to be interrogated further. The most significant "social microcosm" in American literature is Herman Melville's *Moby-Dick* (1851) in which rich and poor, Caucasians and people of color gather on

9

Scientists believe they have found life on Mars in "Smile, You're on Mars Camera" (October 7, 1965).

the *Pequod* to chase a lucrative career in whaling. With the Civil War looming, Melville argued that the ship of state would sink unless Americans shed their absurd belief in racist science. In a remarkable moment in New Bedford, Ishmael gets into bed with Pacific Islander Queequeg, turns to him, and remarks that this man reminds him of George Washington. In one stroke, Melville destroys the nineteenth-century eugenic belief in the racial superiority of white people.

While the natives who show up on *Gilligan's Island* are racist caricatures, especially when compared to Melville's startling nineteenth-century antiracist stance, it is also true that there were no women allowed on the *Pequod*. That is to say, there are clear deficiencies in both texts when read through present-day values. However, the linkages between *Gilligan's Island* and *Moby-Dick* are also important. Gilligan is Schwartz's Ishmael, a naïf who leads us through the 1960s. However, Gilligan is not one to mutter about the "damp, drizzly November in my soul" (Melville 3)—he's more of a dry, sunny March sort of a chap—because Schwartz no longer needs to tilt at nineteenth-century windmills. The civil rights movement had pushed America into a radical social revolution. So instead of Melville's iconoclastic stance against racism, Schwartz's microcosm retreats from direct social strife. *Gilligan's Island* offers a utopia that deliberately insists on the superiority of its simplicity to the chaos back on the mainland. I offer no apology for *Gilligan's Island*'s political limitations—the Pacific Islanders are regrettable stereotypes, and the gender roles of Mary Ann and Ginger replicate the virgin/whore dynamic of Western civilization—but instead suggest that there are other frameworks to understand the show's grappling with American society and its foibles.

Whereas Melville needs his microcosm to sink in order to demonstrate the deadly path being chosen by nineteenth-century Americans, Schwartz needs his island to stay afloat and isolated in order to keep alive a dream of a better America. To the extent that his show continues to delight around the world in syndication, Schwartz continues to succeed in this mission. From the perspective of globalization, *Gilligan's Island* unequivocally offers a better America than the one we actually have. In real life, both in the 1960s and today, America projects its military power around the world. In the diegesis of *Gilligan's Island,* military power washes up on the island and mostly terrorizes the castaways with radiation and munitions. For example, in "Splashdown" (season 3, episode 90, February 20, 1967), the castaways believe a NASA space capsule that crashes on the island might be their key to rescue. However, NASA decides that they cannot afford to have the capsule and its top secret equipment fall into the hands of the Soviet Union. When all the castaways secretly hide on the capsule to get rescued, it begins to sink in the lagoon. They abandon the vessel just as NASA blows it up. The castaways triumph over such assaults largely through the MacGyver-like skills of the Professor and his coconut-based laboratory. Conversely, extradiegetically, *Gilligan's Island* itself is exported around the world, a comedy of seven loving humans that is unequivocally a better gift to the people of Guam and Nigeria than General Electric's nuclear weapons.

Schwartz and his writers directly invoke *Moby-Dick* only once. As "Mine Hero" (season 2, episode 50, December 23, 1965) begins, Gilligan gets a huge bite on his fishing pole at the lagoon. He enthuses to the Skipper, "Maybe it's Moby-Dick!" However, Gilligan catches not a fish but a mine. Gilligan's pole activates one of the mine's probes, which begins ticking ominously. When the Professor examines the mine, he becomes concerned: the island's subterranean pockets of gas could threaten the whole island. If the mine explodes, so could the island. Thus, like the threat Ahab's mad quest and his whale quarry pose to the *Pequod,* so too does the Moby-Dick mine imperil Schwartz's microcosm.

However, unlike Ishmael, who merely witnesses the destruction of the American microcosm at the hands of Moby-Dick, Gilligan's bravery saves his friends. The Professor loads the mine on a raft to tow it out to sea where it cannot do any damage when it explodes. As the Professor and the Skipper draw lots as to who will do the dangerous job, Gilligan, fearing for his friends' lives, paddles in fast motion. Because his good luck charm is magnetic, the mine is attracted to Gilligan and floats out to sea behind him. After Gilligan paddles onto the shore, the mine explodes at sea, delivering to the castaways a sumptuous shower of exploded fish. Thus, Gilligan as Ishmael takes direct action to protect his American microcosm from the 1960s white whale—deadly military technology. In some odd combination of the Old and New Testaments, Gilligan makes it rain not frogs but fish; Gilligan himself, in the tradition of Jesus, is a fisher of men, drawing his community together via his selflessness.

12

The relationship of the sinking of the *Pequod* to *Gilligan's Island* is of particular significance for analyzing the episode "Quick, before It Sinks" (season 2, episode 42, October 28, 1965). The episode begins gravely, with the Professor declaring, "The condemned will eat a hearty meal." He has been using a stick to measure the height of the water in the lagoon, and the level has been steadily increasing, causing him to conclude that the island is sinking into the Pacific Ocean. The men are reluctant to tell the women about their doom, but once Ginger, Mary Ann, and Mrs. Howell learn the truth, they immediately form a rescue plan: they will build an ark. To test the plan, the Professor builds an apparatus to test the design of their new ship, the SS *Minnow II*.

The episode to this point is biblically Melvillean; the intertextual reference to Noah frames the watery demise of the American social microcosm. However, unlike Melville, Schwartz and his writers have in mind a comic turn. In a parody of Charlie Chaplin's *The Immigrant* (1915), Gilligan and the Skipper sit down inside the Professor's apparatus to attempt to eat while at sea. Whereas the furniture is secured, the food is not, so it flies all over the room. At one point, Gilligan stabs Skipper's hand with a fork, missing his food entirely. At another, Gilligan pours coconut milk all over the Skipper, missing his glass by a full 90 degrees.

The comic turn is justified in the episode's coda. It turns out the castaways never need the *Minnow II*. Gilligan brings in his lobster traps; he has been using the Professor's measuring stick to gauge the depth of the water into which he places his traps. Since the lobster fishing yields have been declining, he has been moving the stick into deeper and deeper water. While Melville's *Moby-Dick* is about the sinking of the *Pequod* as a result of Ahab's mad mission that dooms his microcosm, *Gilligan's Island* finds the American representatives safe and sound on terra firma. The sinking of Schwartz's social microcosm is only dangled as a plot device but, within twenty-three minutes, is dismantled by the comic impulse.

13

In these early forays into analyzing *Gilligan's Island*, I have mixed with wild abandon two intertextual readings of the show, one claiming its relationship to absurdist comedy in *Waiting for Godot* and the other its Melvillean exploration of American cultural identity. The method for this book is built on the belief that the ninety-eight episodes of *Gilligan's Island*, each in their own way, couple with a great diversity of texts in the Western tradition in such productive, intellectually stimulating ways.

Studying Gilligan

Whatever else it may be, *Gilligan's Island* is one of the most ubiquitously comprehended references in American cultural history. An extended study via Google Books bears witness to this grandiose claim. The largest group of *Gilligan's Island* hits in Google's massive collection of scanned books is in novels: characters mention sitting around watching reruns of the sitcom, usually to express some form of self-loathing for their own time-wasting proclivities. For example, the narrator of Scott

Michael Gallagher's novel *Geneva* (2007) writes:

> Long before I met Geneva, the nighttime had a dual aspect for me. Being an insomniac, many nights were filled with the horrors of restlessness—watching late night cable, with its surreal infomercials, *I Dream of Jeannie* or *Gilligan's Island* reruns etc.—a maddening and torturous twilight zone of loneliness and frustration in which time took on the slow tick of suffering as my body begged for the relief of sleep while I channel surfed on the couch. (216)

The other citations, in academic works, argue directly against this notion of the show as a complete waste of time, positioning *Gilligan's Island* within a wide intellectual terrain. Priscilla Walton begins her study of cannibalism with reference to the show: "Like many other 1960s children, I saw my first 'cannibal' on television. As a regular viewer of the TV program *Gilligan's Island,* each week I watched the trials of the protagonists, who were stranded on a desert island where they were periodically visited by cannibalistic headhunters" (1). In their communication textbook, Tony Schirato and Susan Yell use the show as their point of reference in order to explain ideology:

> From a Marxist perspective, everything that happens on the island can (more or less) be explained in terms of the actions of Mr. Howell and his capitalist operations. But as we have seen, there are many competing identities and ideologies on *Gilligan's Island.* How can we make sense of this? Volosinov makes the point that economics is just one of a number of spheres we have to take into account. . . . The professor and Mr. Howell . . . are taking part in an ideological struggle involving different types of habitus, and therefore different values, goals and agendas. (79–80)

Schirato and Yell use *Gilligan's Island* in a similar way that I do in my classroom, as a cultural reference that one can be sure students know well. As a teacher, I believe that if we want students to grasp complicated analytical material, it is best to apply these methods, not to difficult high culture, but instead to texts with which they already have a significant familiarity.

Despite the ubiquitous popular mastery of *Gilligan's Island*—or perhaps precisely because of it—the show is the most ignored text in television studies proper. Indeed, up until just a few years ago, there was not one critical article in film and television studies devoted to the show, this in a discipline in which studying *Buffy the Vampire Slayer* (UPN/WB, 1997–2003) has become a career choice. Often when the show is invoked by serious scholarship, it is presented as a negative case, an example of television at its most inane. In *Watching TV*, Harry Castleman and Walter Podrazik typify the critical presentation of the show as repetitive, mindless drivel: "The program that showcased Aubrey escapism at its worst was *Gilligan's Island*, which followed the adventures of the passengers and crew of a sight-seeing charter boat that was shipwrecked on an uncharted South Pacific island. The show literally went to the ends of the earth to avoid reality in a premise that seemed to overwhelm the writers with its limitations" (173). James Aubrey was president of CBS network television in the 1960s, generally associated with frivolous, anti-intellectual programming—"broads, bosoms, and fun" (Grossman 68)—and was often in conflict with aesthete William Paley, who prided himself on his art collection (perhaps because of which he also loved making money, which *Gilligan's Island* did, in large piles). Castleman and Podrazik's invocation of Aubrey to critique the show is more than a bit ironic, since Schwartz constantly fought with this head of CBS programming over *Gilligan's Island*, Aubrey's idea being that the show should be more like *Wagon Train* in which Gilligan and the Skipper would give boat rides to new tourists every week, a kind of 1960s *Fantasy Island* (ABC, 1977–84). Nonetheless, to

15

this day, *Gilligan's Island* stands as a marker of the worst of tele-vision's banality for academic critics devoted to the medium. In his recent defense of *Lost* (ABC, 2004–10), Jason Mittell argues, "Like many, I approached *Lost* with frames of reference of other deserted-on-an-island narratives, from *Lord of the Flies* to *Survivor* (or if it turned out to be a true disaster, *Gilligan's Island*)."

Ironically, for a show so resolutely tied to popular culture, academic Shakespeareans are the one group of critics who have attended sympathetically to *Gilligan's Island*. In a much-beloved episode, "The Producer" (season 3, episode 72, October 3, 1966), comedian Phil Silvers guest stars as Broadway producer Harold Hecuba, who arrives on the island in an attempt to get away from civilization and restore his lost creativity. Trying to impress Hecuba with the acting talent of Hollywood starlet Ginger, the castaways put on a musical version of William Shakespeare's *Hamlet* (1604), setting the tragedy to the tunes of Georges Bizet's *Carmen* (1875) and Jacques Offenbach's *Tales of Hoffmann* (1881). In *Unspeakable ShaXXXspeares: Queer Theory and American Kiddie Culture,* Richard Burt argues, "Vocal and visual transvestism is at the center of a contest between an individualistic model of literary authorship as appropriation (the Producer) and a collaborative model of literary production as the joint recycling of available cultural resources (the castaways)" (170–71). In his short, one hundred–page analysis of *Hamlet* for the Landmarks of World Literature series, Paul Cantor finds room to include a discussion of this episode: "It is doubtful that the writers of this show (Gerald Gardner and Dee Caruso) realized that they were working within a long tradition of *Hamlet* parodies that stretches back into the nineteenth century, and yet the resemblance of their work to the plays [Stanley] Wells [author of the five-volume *Nineteenth-Century Shakespeare Burlesques*] reprints is uncanny" (92).

In a separate work, *Gilligan Unbound: Pop Culture in the Age of Globalization,* Cantor has produced the only extended study of *Gilligan's Island* in the academic literature. In a wonderful book resolutely ignored by mainstream television studies, Cantor compares two utopian shows from the 1960s (*Gilligan's Island* and *Star Trek* [NBC, 1966–69]) with two dystopian ones from the 1990s (*The Simpsons* [Fox, 1989–present] and *The X-Files* [Fox, 1993–2002]), thus building a model for the historical collapse of American democratic ideals while simultaneously writing quite brilliantly about four of the most accomplished and important shows in the history of television. Throughout his chapter "The Courage of the Fearless Crew: *Gilligan's Island* and the Americanization of the Globe," Cantor carefully details the show's varied episodes, calling attention to feminism ("St. Gilligan and the Dragon" [season 1, episode 20, February 13, 1965] in which the female castaways secede from patriarchy); to modernist narrative ("Diogenes, Won't You Please Go Home?" [season 1, episode 31, May 1, 1965], told via contradictory flashbacks, a method inspired by *Rashomon* [Akira Kurosawa, 1950]); and to the Cold War ("The Little Dictator" [season 2, episode 39, September 30, 1965] in which Gilligan dreams he is a South American dictator).

This book follows Cantor's preliminary study by attending to the variety of aesthetic, narrative, and ideological material present in the ninety-eight episodes of *Gilligan's Island*. However, the Shakespearean roots of the prior work on the show have occluded its dominant obsession—performativity. While many sitcoms are, by definition, self-reflexive examinations of the performative nature of television stars (Lucy's endless attempts to break into show business or the representation of domestic life on *The Dick Van Dyke Show* [CBS, 1961–66] as the grist mill for the writing of a variety comedy show), the striking thing about *Gilligan's Island* is that, for no apparent reason whatsoever, the castaways find themselves, episode after episode, performing, in all senses of the word. In one episode, "High Man on the Totem Pole" (season 3, episode 91, February 27, 1967), Gilligan has to protect the castaways from headhunters by playing the part of an island god. In another, "The

17

Second Ginger Grant" (season 3, episode 92, March 6, 1967), Mary Ann gets amnesia and believes she is in fact Ginger Grant. For the rest of the episode, Ginger has to playact as Mary Ann in order not to threaten her confused friend's mental health.

The centrality of performativity in *Gilligan's Island* would not, of course, have been possible without great performers. The show is exquisitely cast, turning away from the axial narrative norms of the sitcom. The song and dance performers in *I Love Lucy,* while very talented, direct their energies inwardly to, well, love Lucy. Many great television performers help write Alan Brady's variety show, but they do so in the context of *The Dick Van Dyke Show.* Despite the show's title, *Gilligan's Island,* the island in fact did not belong to any of the seven performers. Causing many ego-induced headaches for Schwartz, each of the cast members clamored for more screen time and individual episodes devoted to their characters.

Bob Denver, who played Gilligan, came to the show with prior sitcom experience. Well known for his role as Maynard G. Krebs on *The Many Loves of Dobie Gillis* (CBS, 1959–63), Denver extended his populist beatnik performance on *Gilligan's Island.* A naïf who shuns corporate work, Maynard-cum-Gilligan finds a life outside of the button-down conventions of 1960s American life. However, *Gilligan's Island* is not an axial sitcom in which the cast only reacts to Gilligan. The other cast members form a utopian community in which each member contributes to life on the island. Alan Hale Jr., as the Skipper, brought a familial Hollywood legacy to the series. The son of Alan Hale, famous as Errol Flynn's loveable Little John in *The Adventures of Robin Hood* (Michael Curtiz, 1938), Alan Hale Jr. began as one of the regulars on Gene Autry's films and television shows in the 1950s. Bringing his father's amiable abilities as a character actor to *Gilligan's Island,* Alan Hale Jr. became beloved as the Skipper, the comedic partner to Gilligan's shenanigans; they were a comic duo in the tradition of Laurel and Hardy and Abbott and Costello.

The other cast members brought equal acting skill in inhabiting their roles on the ensemble comedy. When he took the role of Thurston Howell III, Jim Backus was already familiar for decades as a wealthy man (as Hubert Updike III on Alan Young's radio show) and as a comically suffering husband, both Bradley Stevens's father on television's *I Married Joan* (NBC, 1952–55) and juvenile delinquent Jim Stark's henpecked father in *Rebel without a Cause* (Nicholas Ray, 1955). Backus would go on to delight further a new generation as the voice of cartoon hero *Mr. Magoo,* a crotchety elder in the spirit of Mr. Howell. "The rest" of the cast brought skillful character acting to the show: Russell Johnson as Professor Roy Hinckley had prior experience in low-budget science fiction films including *It Came from Outer Space* (Jack Arnold, 1953), while Natalie Schaffer as Mrs. Howell had appeared in dozens of Hollywood films in the 1940s and 1950s as second-banana beautiful sophisticates in films such as *Forever Darling* (Alexander Hall, 1956).

Thus, what the Shakespeareans have missed by only focusing on the connections between *Hamlet* and *Gilligan's Island* is that the show is more generally about the radical importance of performativity for human sustenance. For not only do the castaways put on a musical version of *Hamlet,* they also produce and act in a silent movie ("Castaways Pictures Presents" [season 2, episode 43, November 4, 1965]); stage the Antony and Cleopatra play that Ginger was supposed to premiere on Broadway ("Angel on the Island" [season 1, episode 11, December 12, 1964]); and reenact a crime in order to prove that no one on the island is a murderer ("Not Guilty" [season 2, episode 52, January 6, 1966]). The show also relies to an unusual extent on a wide array of intertextual reenactments via dream sequences, among fans the most memorable and enjoyable of all of the episodes of *Gilligan's Island*: "The Sound of Quacking" (season 1, episode 7, November 7, 1964) was shot on the set of *Gunsmoke,* producing a *High Noon* (Fred Zinnemann, 1952) parody featuring the castaways in a western; "And Then There

The Professor desperately tries to fix the radio, the castaways' only link to the mainland, in "Goodnight Sweet Skipper" (10/17/64)

Were None" (season 3, episode 81, December 5, 1966) features Gilligan as Dr. Jekyll and Mr. Hyde; and "Up at Bat" (season 3, episode 69, September 12, 1966) involves Gilligan dreaming he is Dracula after having been bitten by what he believes to be a vampire bat. In this book, I will explore the unique way in which *Gilligan's Island* constructed American identity as especially performative and malleable.

An Industrial History of *Gilligan's Island*

Gilligan's Island is the archetype of the 1960s telefilm sitcom. Shot almost exclusively on a soundstage in Los Angeles, the show from its first broadcast suffered the scorn of critics everywhere. The reviewer for the *L.A. Times* argued, "*Gilligan's Island* is a show that should never have reached the airwaves, this season or any other" (qtd. in Bathroom Reader's Institute 38). The *San Francisco Chronicle* notice was even more blunt: "It is difficult to believe that this show was written, directed, and produced by adults. It marks a new low in the networks' estimation of public intelligence" (qtd. in Bathroom Reader's Institute 38). At first glance, the ending of "Gilligan Goes Gung-Ho"—in which Sheriff Gilligan locks all the castaways into a cave for minor offenses, thus making it impossible for them to signal a passing search plane—seems to provide perfect evidence for the reductive narrative of which the show is so often accused: yet again, Gilligan does something stupid, and yet again, the castaways are improbably stuck on the island, "as primitive as can be."

Yet *Gilligan's Island* is a far more complicated text than the attacks on its formulaic reductionism would indicate. Clearly an example of television in the era of "the vast wasteland," *Gilligan's Island* is also an intelligent response to such a critique of television's childish imbecility. The era from which the show emerges is named, of course, after John F. Kennedy's FCC commissioner Newton Minow's 1961 speech at the National Association of Broadcasters' annual conference challenging owners of affiliated stations to watch their programming for just one day without going mad at its inanity. *Gilligan's Island* most famously in its naming of the castaways' wrecked boat, the SS *Minnow,* provided Sherwood Schwartz with a vessel for arguing against the FCC commissioner's elitism, the extra *n* in the boat version of the commissioner's name perhaps identifying him most directly as a smelly fish. Schwartz has many times expressed his anger at Minow's elitist policies, most frequently in his book, *Inside* Gilligan's Island (xv, 5).

Gilligan's Island proposes that popular culture might just be the correct vehicle for social analysis (as Schwartz argued by pitching the show to CBS head William Paley as a "social microcosm"). Shakespeare scholar Paul Cantor analyzes the reductionism of *Gilligan's Island* quite differently than the show's contemporary newspaper critics: "When one adds up all the characters who come to the island from mainland civilization, it becomes clear that the castaways are better off where they are. Neither too primitive nor too corrupted by modern civilization, they are free to lead a virtuous democratic existence on their island" (*Gilligan Unbound* 22).

When one goes back to look at the *Gilligan's Island* pilot, one can see the logic of the original critics' arguments. In the pilot accepted by CBS Television, which Schwartz disavows because it was edited out of his control, more time is spent on the preparations for the voyage, since the network refused to allow the use of Schwartz's theme song for the production of the pilot. Instead, a Caribbean singer narrates the shipwreck story in a different song. Also, the characters are less defined, with Bunny (Nancy McCarthy, who would be replaced by Dawn Wells playing Mary Ann) and Ginger (Kit Smythe) both similarly ditzy secretaries. The comedy of the pilot (which was not aired until TBS showed it on October 16, 1992, with an introduction by Bob Denver) is flat at best. The episode features some gags on which the show's comedy would be built: for example, the Professor fixes the boat's radio transmitter only to have Gilligan cast it out to sea accidentally with his fishing pole. There is one very funny sequence in which Gilligan catches a fish that has swallowed the radio. The audio device improbably keeps working: the castaways listen to Roger Maris playing baseball. When the castaways begin talking into the fish's mouth just in case it also swallowed the transmitter, the Howells walk by thinking their compatriots have gone mad. However, in all, the unaired pilot for *Gilligan's Island* is lackluster and not at all predictive of the intelligent show it would become.

Indeed, the entire first season of *Gilligan's Island* is very different than the subsequent two seasons on which I focus much of my analysis in this book. When three test screenings of various versions of the pilot preferred by the studio failed miserably, Schwartz was able to recut the pilot to his liking. Despite featuring the comic timing preferred by Schwartz, the aired pilot, "Two on a Raft" (September 24, 1964), is little better than the unaired version. The episode begins the morning after the shipwreck, as the castaways awaken to discover their circumstances on the island. Thinking he is still at sea, Gilligan jumps awake and dives overboard, only to land face first into the sand. Gilligan and the Skipper set sail on a makeshift raft while the other castaways (now featuring Russell Johnson as the Professor, Tina Louise as Ginger, and Dawn Wells as Mary Ann) search the island, fearing the presence of Marubi headhunters. When their raft sinks, Gilligan and the Skipper unknowingly end up on the very same island from which they sailed. They and the other castaways mistake one another's sounds for the Marubi. The episode ends with a comic bit about a spring trap above a cave entrance. Each set of castaways enters the cave, fighting with each other in the dark, thinking they are Marubi. After Gilligan accidentally springs the trap, sealing all seven castaways into the cave, they dig themselves out amicably as the episode comes to an end.

The Narrative Innovations of *Gilligan's Island*

The first season of *Gilligan's Island* is far more devoted to serial narrative than we would expect of a 1960s telefilm sitcom. In episode 2, "Home Sweet Hut" (October 3, 1964), the Skipper demands that each of the castaways help build huts for protection. When everyone wants their own hut, the castaways have to work together to settle on how they can most efficiently protect themselves from the elements. Even by the end of this episode, the castaways have not settled on the solution yet, as each castaway sets off to build his or her own hut. Eventually, Gilligan and Skipper would bunk together, as would Mr. and

Mrs. Howell, and Mary Ann and Ginger, leaving the Professor to inhabit the supply hut alone. In episode 3, "Voodoo Something to Me" (October 10, 1964), the Skipper's irrational fear of the supernatural powers of the Pacific Islanders is introduced, a fear that would return again and again in the series. In "Voodoo" (season 3, episode 73, October 10, 1966), one of the most beloved episodes of the series, a witch doctor constructs cute voodoo dolls of all the castaways.

In episode 12 ("Birds Gotta Fly, Fish Gotta Talk," December 19, 1964), a Christmas episode, the castaways decorate a tree while reminiscing about their first day on the island. This allowed Schwartz to once again edit the footage shot for the pilot, refining that material yet again. All of these early episodes demonstrate the care the first season spent on telling the story of the castaways on the island. By the middle of the first season,

The Witch Doctor's voodoo doll castaways in "Voodoo" (October 10, 1966).

these sorts of stories would be depleted, forcing the writers of the show into the absurdist minimalism I argue is the productive heart of the show.

The best example of this shift lies in the show's increasing reliance on dream sequences. Of the ninety-eight episodes of *Gilligan's Island,* fourteen of them featured act 2 dream sequences exactly seven minutes in length. Typically, Gilligan would go to sleep worrying about the events of the day, and his subconscious mind would process that material into a familiar story (*Dracula, Cinderella,* and the like). Season 1 featured only three such dream sequences. In the most interesting episode, "The Sound of Quacking," the dream sequence allowed the crew to shoot on the set of *Gunsmoke* and was thus primarily an industrial, not a thematic, decision. After obsessing about eating fish and bananas for weeks, the castaways capture a duck that lands on the island. Gilligan goes to sleep cradling Everett, the name he chooses for the duck, protecting the tasty fowl from the other ravenous castaways. As Gilligan enters his dream state, he emerges as Marshal Dillon, with Skipper as his assistant, Festus. As in *High Noon,* a mob (Mr. Howell and the Professor) comes to eat the duck, Mrs. Howell plays a shady señora, and Miss Ginger comes to seduce Gilligan. Awaking from his dream, Gilligan finds the duck missing and thinks the castaways ate him. Instead, the duck has wandered off, eating berries that the Professor had previously believed to be poisonous. The castaways, delighted they now have a food source, agree to send the duck for help. However, Gilligan again keeps them from getting rescued when he forgets to tie the message for help to the duck's leg before sending it off on its flight to the mainland.

As the possibilities for generating serial narrative about the castaways' daily experiences on the island dwindled, by seasons 2 and 3 the writers increased the frequency of dream sequences. In doing so, they created some of the most memorable episodes of *Gilligan's Island.* Despite still being shot on minimalist sets, the actors on the show recall these episodes the most fondly, as the gimmick allowed them to explore different aspects of the characters than was allowed during the regular sections of the show on the island. In season 2, the five dream sequences include "The Little Dictator" in which Gilligan dreams he is a Latin American dictator; "The Postman Cometh" (episode 54, January 20, 1966) in which the castaways take on the roles of Mary Ann's favorite soap opera characters; and "V for Vitamins" (episode 66, April 14, 1966), which retells the story of Jack and the Beanstalk.

Season 3 would further intensify the importance of the dream sequence narrative. Six of the thirty episodes of the final season used the dream sequence structure. These episodes were the most aggressively built on parody of all the show's dream sequences, including "Up at Bat," the season 3 opener in which Gilligan becomes Dracula; "The Invasion" (episode 79, November 21, 1966), a funny James Bond spoof similar to *Get Smart* (NBC/CBS, 1965–70); "And Then There Were None," a Robert Louis Stephenson parody in which the screaming of "fresh fish" turns Gilligan from Dr. Jekyll into Mr. Hyde; "Court-Martial" (episode 85, January 9, 1967), a swashbuckler parody of Errol Flynn pirate movies; "Lovey's Secret Admirer" (episode 87, January 23, 1967), where Mrs. Howell is Cinderella; and "The Secret of Gilligan's Island" (episode 93, March 13, 1967) in which we see the castaways as primitives on the island in prehistoric times.

The dream sequences are the most identifiable narrative innovation of *Gilligan's Island* and something for which the show is easily recognizable even by casual viewers. Despite their reductionism (they are all exactly seven minutes in length, many of them are shot on bare soundstages with a smoke machine), the dream sequences ironically provide much of the show's inventiveness, because they allowed the characters to get off the island and the actors to try out different performance styles.

Gilligan's Island is caught between the two primary narrative traditions of the sitcom, as analyzed by David Barker. On the

The Professor charts the castaways' ocean voyage in "The Secret of Gilligan's Island" (March 13, 1967).

one hand, it is an axial narrative, like *I Love Lucy* before it or *All in the Family* (CBS, 1971–79) after. Archie and his chair is the center around which Norman Lear's stories orbit; the island is named after Gilligan, not the other castaways. In the first season credit sequence, the Professor and Mary Ann were famously sung about as merely "the rest"; indeed, all six castaways were the rest to Gilligan.

On the other hand, *Gilligan's Island* is a very early attempt at an ensemble narrative in the sitcom, akin to *M*A*S*H* (CBS, 1972–83). With seven characters representing competing interests—in Richard Linklater's *Dazed and Confused* (1993), journalism students analyze the castaways as the seven deadly sins (Gilligan as sloth, Skipper as anger, Mr. Howell as gluttony,

Mrs. Howell as vanity, Mary Ann as envy, Ginger as lust, and the Professor as pride)—Schwartz was able to recombine plotlines with wild abandon. One episode could explore Mary Ann's love of soap operas, whereas another could feature the Professor's scientific work on the island. That is to say, its vast wasteland telefilm status notwithstanding, *Gilligan's Island* was a bold narrative experiment that combined the axial and ensemble traditions of the sitcom.

Gilligan's Cave

The comic simplicity of *Gilligan's Island* was deliberately offered as a parody of Cold War liberal Newton Minow's elitist critique of "mindless" early 1960s television. This critique was built into the very name of the sunken boat that marooned the castaways, the *Minnow*. However, *Gilligan's Island* was not simply apolitical trash. The show's very interest in establishing a utopian island outside of mainstream representational techniques made it a distinctly political show, for which "Gilligan Goes Gung-Ho" is just one of the best examples.

The imposition of law and order on the utopian island results in the castaways missing their chance at rescue once again. The ending of "Gilligan Goes Gung-Ho" serves not only as an ideal defense of popular culture—the most visible 1960s critique of law and order is not found in some countercultural Joseph Heller novel but instead on archconservative William Paley's CBS television network—but also as an object lesson in practical pedagogy.

One of the foundational texts of Western political philosophy is, of course, Plato's *Republic* (380 BCE). In the book, Plato suggests the best path for human governance. The most ubiquitous pedagogical lesson in *Republic* is book 7, which begins with the "Allegory of the Cave." In this familiar story, a man escapes from chains inside a cave where he has only been al-

28

lowed to see two-dimensional shadows on a wall. Outside, he discovers a three-dimensional world filled with light. When the man returns to his compatriots chained inside the cave, they resist his teaching, since he is assaulting the very nature of life as they know it. Plato uses the story to argue for the benefits of enlightened education, but also to warn of the dangers to those who try to enlighten those who live in darkness. Given the ubiquity of caves on *Gilligan's Island,* it seems likely that Plato's cave is part of the intertextual fabric of Schwartz's plan. His show is a kind of popular culture republic, showing 1960s Americans an enlightened way of life every week on a fictional tropical paradise. The thwarting of the rescue at the end of "Gilligan Goes Gung-Ho" does not just happen in any location, but in Plato's cave.

The episode "Hi-Fi Gilligan" (season 2, episode 46, November 25, 1965) offers a particularly emotionally moving use of the enlightenment motif of Plato's cave. As the episode begins, the castaways are preparing for a typhoon to hit the island. Gilligan and the Skipper carry boxes of provisions into a cave that the Professor has deemed solid enough to survive the storm. However, through slapstick comic high jinks, the Skipper accidentally hits Gilligan over the head with a crate, hurting his jaw. When Gilligan opens his mouth, it plays music as if it were a radio.

The Professor examines Gilligan's mouth, concluding that the boy has become a radio receiver due to the accident: one of his molars is now in contact with a silver filling, thus completing a radio circuit in Gilligan's head. Skipper jokes, "Wouldn't it be great if my little buddy could be turned into a color TV?" This of course is close to the truth: after a first season in black and white, season 2 found Gilligan beaming into people's homes as a color television image at long last.

After much comic hilarity about Gilligan interfering with their radio reception, the castaways learn of the imminent approach of the typhoon. They all rush into the cave. However,

29

between the stockpile of provisions and all seven bodies, they cannot possibly squish into its cramped confines. Even after taking out all of the supplies, still only six people can fit. Skipper tries to be brave, ordering his six friends to save themselves in the cave. However, no one obeys this directive. The Professor then suggests they draw straws. Seemingly, Gilligan unluckily chooses the short straw. He goes outside and holds onto a tree with all of his might. Inside the cave, the Skipper realizes that Gilligan tricked them, only pretending to have the shortest straw. Skipper announces to his friends that Gilligan is too important to be left alone; he goes to join his little buddy out at the tree, putting his arms around his waist. One by one, all of the castaways abandon the cave to be with Gilligan during the storm. At the precise moment that all seven castaways have joined arms, lightning strikes the cave, destroying it. Through his prime act of unselfishness, Gilligan has saved his friends. In turn, by loving Gilligan, they have saved themselves. This episode conveys the importance of community in American social life in as precise a way as possible.

So profound is this episode's basic humanity, it was reworked by *The Simpsons* in the episode "Bart's Comet" (season 6, episode 117, February 5, 1995). Ned Flanders has built a bomb shelter in his backyard. When a comet that Bart discovers plummets directly toward the town of Springfield, Homer weasels his way into the shelter, having refused to plan ahead for Armageddon as the paranoid right-wing Christian has. Eventually, most of the rest of the town, equally as unprepared as Homer, forces itself into Ned's family's small bomb shelter. Unable to stand up and say no to his pushy neighbors, Ned and his family go outside. Seeing this, and suddenly finding his humanity, Homer goes outside to be with Flanders. The rest of the town follows and is saved when the comet burns up in the atmosphere, leaving one small rock large enough to destroy only the bomb shelter at impact. *Gilligan's Island* and its legacy sitcom, *The Simpsons,* both devise a simple allegory to teach the importance of community over individualism. By setting the allegory in a cave, *Gilligan's Island* built this lesson televisually on the bedrock of Platonic philosophy. In the first season, the show would apply this ancient backdrop to contemporary problems, including the legacy of World War II for American social life.

The Skipper's War Trauma

In a way that seems surprising in 2011, the politics of the first season of *Gilligan's Island* focus on the legacy of World War II. Season 1 of *Gilligan's Island* does not conceive of World War II as history; it is present for the characters and still being fought on the island. Nineteen years after the end of the war in the Pacific, the characters—particularly the Skipper—and the island itself are haunted by that conflict. Most intriguingly, episode 4, "Goodnight, Sweet Skipper" (October 17, 1964), engages the psychology of war trauma. The episode's teaser begins with the Skipper sleepwalking. Having been at war as a navy sailor on a sub-chasing destroyer, the Skipper goes to the lagoon in order to convert the radio into a transmitter. Using Gilligan's finger as a screwdriver, the somnambulant Skipper fails to fix the imaginary device, ordering his men to abandon ship because of the incoming Japanese dive-bombers. Gilligan, used to obeying orders, dives into the lagoon, thus comically returning to and altering the opening joke of the pilot in which Gilligan dove onto dry land thinking he was still at sea.

Act 1 of the episode begins the next morning, when the Skipper recalls that his dream was set during the Battle of Guadalcanal. Since an Amelia Earhart–style female pilot is flying around the world, and luckily over the island soon, the Professor tries desperately to get the Skipper to remember how to convert the radio into a transmitter (why the Professor, a 1960s MacGyver, does not know how to do this himself, is not made clear). The castaways desperately try to get the Skipper to sleepwalk again so that his subconscious mind will release the occluded transmitter repair knowledge. Gilligan keeps interrupting the Skipper's sleep, so the Professor hypnotizes the sea captain. The rest of the castaways portray the Skipper's men on Guadalcanal, playacting various sailors and surreptitiously supplying the necessary battle noises to convince the Skipper of the realism of the situation. This performance seems to work; the Professor thinks he learns how to fix the transmitter, however, it still does not work. Exhausted, the other castaways go to bed, leaving Gilligan fiddling with the radio. After hitting it in frustration, it comes to life, allowing Gilligan to talk with the pilot flying overhead, but he is not able to give her their exact position. He runs off to get the Skipper, but when he hits the radio again to show him how he got it to work, he breaks it for good. The Skipper is convinced that Gilligan dreamed the whole episode.

Obsessively, the individual episodes of the first season of *Gilligan's Island* return to the representation of war trauma. In the fifteenth episode, "So Sorry, My Island Now" (January 9, 1965), the legacy of World War II is not psychological but physical. In the episode's teaser segment, we see a Japanese sailor emerge from the lagoon in a one-man submarine. While Gilligan runs off to warn the Professor and Skipper, the Japanese sailor takes Mr. Howell prisoner. One by one, the soldier captures the castaways. In a makeshift brig, the Professor tries to explain to the combatant that the war has been over for twenty years. The soldier explains that his radio broke in 1942.

Based on a real story of Japanese soldiers continuing to fight on remote Pacific islands long after the war was over, the episode is remarkable in its complexity. While a racist stereotype straight out of U.S. World War II propaganda (such as the vile Warner Bros. cartoon, *Bugs Bunny Nips the Nips* [1943]), the Japanese soldier is well trained in American culture. He went to UCLA, which annoys Mr. Howell, who believes even Yale is beneath his Harvard education, but nevertheless makes him well conversant with American civilization. He discusses movie stars with Ginger; he emulates Rod Taylor, Robert Montgomery, and Lloyd Bridges. Indeed, he admits that he learned to construct grenades from American movies featuring John Wayne.

The World War II arc concludes season 1 of *Gilligan's Island*. In episode 30, "Forget Me Not" (April 24, 1965), another fifteen episodes into the show, Gilligan accidentally knocks the Skipper over the head during a semaphore demonstration in an attempt to signal a passing ship. As a result, Skipper develops amnesia. To cure him, the Professor hypnotizes the Skipper, telling him to "go back to the good old days." After Skipper sees the castaways as kids, the Professor has him grow up faster. "The years are passing; you come to an island in the South Pacific." He now sees the castaways as Japanese soldiers. "I'm surrounded by the enemy," he screams as he rushes into the jungle. The Skipper runs around the island, spying on his friends, whom he mistakes for the enemy. The sailor grabs a gun with a bayonet and holds Mary Ann and Ginger prisoner in a jail cell he has specially constructed in a cave. The sailor again thinks he is on Guadalcanal during the war. Thus, after initially rendering the Skipper's war trauma purely psychological, then showing the Japanese soldier continuing to fight the war in actuality, the World War II arc ends with a synthesis of the two: Skipper is now continuing to fight the war, but through a mistaken identification of his friends as Japanese soldiers.

In serial fashion, the very next episode, "Diogenes, Won't You Please Go Home?," revisits these depictions of war trauma. By ironically activating *Rashomon*, a Japanese film about feudal warfare, the episode foregrounds the instability of human memory in detailing the facts of war heroism. In the episode, the other castaways have become obsessed by what Gilligan might be writing about them in his diary. The episode develops into a series of false recollections of the Japanese soldier incident from the previous week, each from one of the castaway's

33

The Skipper imagines his friends as enemy Japanese soldiers in "Forget Me Not" (April 24, 1965).

unreliable narrational point of view. In Mr. Howell's version, the millionaire got captured on purpose. As the Japanese soldier lines up Gilligan against a wall to shoot him, Mr. Howell rescues Gilligan using only a whip, dancing a tango with the soldier, and defeating him by throwing him into the lagoon. Similarly, Ginger has been writing a film script about the events in which she is a secret agent judo expert who throws the soldier to the ground repeatedly in order to subdue him.

All of the castaways feel horrible when Mary Ann finds Gilligan's diary in the lagoon, where he has thrown it in disgust. In his writing, Gilligan has said all wonderful things about his friends on the island. In the episode's coda, the castaways all burn their journals. Lamenting their inferiority to Gilligan, the

Professor pronounces solemnly, "We see us as we are, but you see us as we would like to be," a stirring tribute to the better angels of our nature.

This simple yet profound lesson in humility is housed in a complex narrative. The *Rashomon* inspiration is focused on a sequence of episodes that demonstrate the lasting impact of World War II. Schwartz here uses the repetition of series television to fold back one episode about the Skipper's post-traumatic stress disorder, another about the Japanese soldier having lost his entire life fighting a long since finished war, and yet a third about the Skipper reenacting the Japanese soldier's continued waging of the war after having been conked on the head. Schwartz waits until the fourth episode in the series, as the first season winds down, to deliver the emotionally compelling moral. Only by returning to the simplicity of Gilligan's worldview in which telling the truth is the key to narration can the castaways, and allegorically the audience, learn to put aside violent self-interest in lieu of the benefits of community. By fusing the first season of the show to the legacy of World War II, Schwartz was thus able to allegorize the United States' role in the Cold War onto a seemingly safe political subject like the Japanese enemy in World War II. By seasons 2 and 3, the show would much more directly engage the Soviet Union as the nation's true enemy.

Gilligan Fights the Cold War

In "Nyet, Nyet—Not Yet" (season 2, episode 45, November 18, 1965), a Soviet space capsule falls into the lagoon. The Professor, above the foibles of political differences, runs to greet the cosmonauts, Igor and Ivan, colonels in the Soviet space program. However, it is in their encounter with Mr. Howell that the cosmonauts engage in the most simplistic fighting of the

Cold War. Igor claims that Mr. Howell is a "capitalist exploiter," which Mr. Howell greets as a fabulous compliment. Not caring at all about ideology, the castaways merely want the cosmonauts to help them get rescued. Alas, the cosmonauts leave the island without telling the Soviet government about the castaways, despite suspecting them of being American colonists of the Pacific Islands. They simply cannot take the risk that their Soviet superiors will come to know of their incompetence. Sure enough, in the episode's coda, the TASS news agency on the radio informs the castaways of the cosmonauts' and Soviet government's cover-up: the capsule did not land off course in the Pacific Ocean but instead eighteen inches from its intended target, in the Black Sea.

Beyond the Cold War, *Gilligan's Island* frequently returned to the theme of war and violence. In "Forward March" (season 2, episode 58, February 17, 1966), the castaways come under attack. During the teaser, someone lobs a grenade at Gilligan and the Skipper. It explodes in a bush just beyond Gilligan's head. After another grenade attack during their argument over whether to surrender or not, the castaways decide to fight back. Ginger volunteers to work as a Mata Hari spy, while Mr. Howell takes over as general, appointing Skipper as secretary of the navy, Gilligan as a private, and Mrs. Howell and Mary Ann as medical nurses.

After being strafed with machine gun fire, the Professor enters the jungle to investigate. He returns with the machine gun, which was oddly abandoned by their enemy, despite being full of ammunition. Mr. Howell concludes that they are dealing with an enemy of superior intelligence. The Professor observes that their opponent is violating all of the principles of guerilla warfare. This turns out to be the organizing joke of the episode; the enemy is not a guerilla, but an actual gorilla. The Professor then observes that the ape must have been on the island during World War II and "figured that was the way humans played with each other." Again, the politics of World War II contaminates the utopia of the island; the violence of human behavior, mimicked by the animal world, now threatens the castaways in the present.

A cave again serves as the episode's place of resolution. The gorilla has two large crates of World War II grenades in a cave. Gilligan, Skipper, and the Professor attempt to steal the grenades from the gorilla but are unsuccessful. Gilligan comes to the rescue, playing a grenade throwing game with the gorilla; as our hero tosses the grenades one by one into the lagoon to dispose of them safely, the gorilla jumps for joy each time. However, once the grenades are all safely exploded, a large red object remains in the box. The gorilla throws that one into the lagoon; this time, the explosion is much larger. A cut reveals that it was an atomic bomb.

This is one of the oddest moments in the entire run of *Gilligan's Island*. Similar to other ridiculous atomic bomb explosions in media texts—in James Cameron's *True Lies* (1994), Harry (Arnold Schwarzenegger) and Helen (Jamie Lee Curtis) repair their marriage by kissing in front of an atomic mushroom cloud off the shores of Florida—the atomic bomb on *Gilligan's Island* does no real harm. The castaways do not suffer the consequences of radiation poisoning as their fellow Pacific Islanders did during U.S. atomic bomb testing in the 1950s. However, Schwartz uses the episode's coda to reflect on the difference between the reality of mutually assured destruction and a fantasy island utopia. When Mr. Howell pins a medal on Gilligan's chest for his bravery during the recent guerilla war, the gorilla has other ideas. He throws a coconut cream pie at Gilligan's face. Whereas the consequences of nuclear war are devastatingly real on the mainlands of the United States and the Soviet Union, on the fantasy island, the worst consequence of the castaways' violence will be a pie fight, that staple of classical Hollywood comedy.

Gilligan and Identity Politics

In terms of current understandings of identity politics, *Gilligan's Island* is least defensible. Its depiction of racial difference is reprehensible: the natives are at once blood thirsty, cannibalistic savages and remarkably incompetent. There is no ethnic diversity among the castaways, even in comparison to a nineteenth-century sea-faring text such as *Moby-Dick*. In terms of social class, the show is facile, demonstrating that even the fabulously wealthy Howells and the working-class Gilligan can come to care about each other intimately. In the episode "The Sweepstakes," Mr. Howell is at first angry at Gilligan's egalitarianism. When Gilligan thinks he has won the lottery, he buys his five friends $50,000 entrance fees into the Howells' formerly exclusive island country club. However, Mr. Howell proves to be more kind than his gruff exterior would at first indicate: even though he knows Gilligan's ticket is two years old, and thus worthless, he still lets all of the castaways participate in country club life. Finally, while the show attends to gender differences, much of its comedy is built on conventional gender roles: Ginger gets her way through seduction, while Mary Ann is stuck doing the cleaning and the cooking.

In one episode, however, "St. Gilligan and the Dragon," an inkling of gender-based critique finds a voice. Shortly after the publication of Betty Friedan's *The Feminine Mystique* (1963), many television sitcoms began grappling with a populist onset of feminism. Most spectacularly, *Bewitched* (ABC, 1964–72) represented the conflict between women as domestic beings and actors in the public space on a weekly basis. Other shows, such as *The Beverly Hillbillies* (CBS, 1964–72) and *Gilligan's Island,* saved such concerns for one or two episodes. In a much later episode arc of *The Beverly Hillbillies,* in 1971, Elly May and Granny stage a feminist protest in Jed's home.

Much earlier on *Gilligan's Island,* the women also go on

strike. In the teaser sequence to "St. Gilligan and the Dragon," the women demand more privacy, refusing to do any more cooking or laundry until the men acknowledge their concerns. "We think that women should have the same rights as men," declares Ginger. The Professor tries to explain rationally: "Historically, it is the men who make the decisions."

Not taking the women seriously, the men laugh at Ginger, Mary Ann, and Mrs. Howell as they leave the encampment to form a women's cooperative on the other side of the island. The episode quickly devolves into a "battle of the sexes" reworking of the "Job Switching" episode of *I Love Lucy* (season 2, episode 39, September 15, 1952). After the men realize that they are incompetent cooks, they seek out the women for reconciliation. When the women see a giant caterpillar in the jungle, they think it is the men trying to play a trick on them. However, they become genuinely frightened when they see that the men have come to apologize. Gilligan beats down the monster with a stick before the Professor can explain that it is a lost weather balloon and that they could repair it to engineer a rescue. By the time the Professor gets to Gilligan, he has completely destroyed the balloon's fragile fabric. In short, at best, *Gilligan's Island* grappled with identity politics in a simplistic way common to 1950s sitcoms such as *I Love Lucy*. Such would not be the case with the show's engagement with the Western literary tradition.

What Great Books Would You Bring to a Desert Island?

As constructed by Sherwood Schwartz, *Gilligan's Island* repeatedly announces itself as existing within, not as opposed to, the literary tradition. *Gilligan's Island* continues the tradition of envisioning a functioning island utopia resistant to the corrupt values of mainland civilization that began with Renaissance (Sir Thomas More) and Enlightenment (Sir Francis Bacon) representations of utopian island communities. The Enlightenment constructions continued into the nineteenth century. Laura Morowitz cites Jules Verne's *The Mysterious Island* (1875) as a source text for *Gilligan's Island.* Quoting Pierre Macherey's essay on Verne, "Jules Verne: The Faulty Narrative," in *A Theory of Literary Production,* Morowitz argues, "The underlying themes of Verne's novels are voyage, scientific invention, and colonization. Such themes come to be embodied, respectively, in the characters of *Gilligan's Island*: the Skipper (voyage), the Professor (invention), and the Howells (colonization)" (118).

Morowitz produces an analysis of the episode "Goodbye, Old Paint" in which an abstract expressionist painter, Alexandri Gregor Dubov, arrives on the island to hide from the modern world and celebrate primitivism in his created artworks. The episode grafts its traditional plot interests—the castaways greet all newcomers to the island as mechanisms of rescue—to an analysis of the cultural status of art. In order to be rescued, the castaways have to pretend that they love Dubov's abstract paintings; they hope this will convince Dubov to return to the mainland, confident he has regained his ability to paint well. Mr. Howell's idea is to lure Dubov into painting the castaways. Ginger attempts to interest Dubov in her services as a model. She claims Picasso and Chagall have already painted her, but that she promised Salvador Dalí that he could be next. Since Dubov hates Dalí, he agrees to paint Ginger as a Bali dancer, but she thinks he has said "belly dancer." After the confusion is cleared up, Dubov produces an abstract version of Ginger made out of geometrical shapes. As part of their scheme to get rescued, rather than indicating their personal scorn for modern art, the castaways enthuse about how wonderful the painting is.

Gilligan lets slip Mr. Howell's plan to Dubov; in reaction, Dubov continues to paint rather than return to the mainland.

The modern painter turns commercial in "Goodbye, Old Paint" (May 22, 1965).

In the second act of the episode, Mr. Howell invents another scheme: they will set up Gilligan as a rival painter to Dubov, in order to get his creative juices flowing. This time, Gilligan in fact delivers the populist critique of modern art: he explains that he painted like Dubov in the third grade, which resulted in a flunking grade from his art teacher. Nonetheless, Gilligan paints; when the other castaways enthusiastically praise Gilligan's painting, Dubov gives Gilligan his transmitter in exchange for painting lessons. Alas, the transmitter is rusted beyond repair. At the episode's end, we learn that Dubov has moved to another island where he intends to continue his primitivist lifestyle. The episode ends with Skipper and Mr. Howell raving about Gilligan's painting, of the huts.

To Be Gilligan, or Not to Be

It is, however, in dialogue with the works of William Shakespeare where *Gilligan's Island* finds its deepest resonance with the traditions of high culture. Despite having been studied intensively by Shakespearean scholars Richard Burt and Paul Cantor, there is still much to be learned from "The Producer" episode of *Gilligan's Island* in which the castaways present a musical version of *Hamlet*. This episode is American culture at its finest, hybridizing an encounter with great literature and setting it within a populist milieu.

The castaways' version of *Hamlet* deconstructs the Shakespeare text, simultaneously delivering a modern, comedic interpretation while teaching a great deal about the nature of Shakespearean performance. Directed by Ida Lupino and George M. Cahan, "The Producer" episode of *Gilligan's Island* demonstrates the fluidity between high and low culture in Schwartz's universe. When Harold Hecuba (Phil Silvers) crash-lands on the island, the castaways believe they can be rescued if they convince the producer to use Ginger in his new musical extravaganza show. The castaways first give Ginger a dinner theater cabaret opportunity to impress Hecuba. As she serves food cooked by Mary Ann, Ginger reenacts various movie roles, first channeling Sophia Loren from *Bitter Rice* (Giuseppe De Santis, 1949). She does an Italian accent, uttering nonsense, confusing the starving people of Italian neorealism with warriors from sword and sandal epics. She blathers on about those "starving on the piazza of Steve Reeves." Hecuba quips: "I think I saw this in a picture once." Next, Ginger comes out to serve Hecuba bread and water, doing a Marilyn Monroe impersonation. When Ginger comes clean—"I just wanted to show you what a versatile actress I was"—Hecuba laughs at her phony accent and overacting. Ginger cries at her failure. The Skipper and Gilligan try to console her, but she is convinced she is going to spend the rest of her life on the island. Act 1 ends with yet another failure of the castaways at a rescue, this time not due to Gilligan but to Ginger's inability to nail her audition.

As act 2 begins, Gilligan saves the day. He believes they should put on a musical to show Hecuba what a wonderful actress Ginger is. The Professor likes Gilligan's idea: the Howells brought records to the island, and they can make a musical adaptation of a book. They look through the books they have. After sorting through all of them, rejecting such titles as *Four-Masted Schooners I Have Known,* the castaways decide on *Hamlet* as their source text. Indicating the vast influence Laurence Olivier's interpretation of the play had on postwar culture, the Professor introduces *Hamlet* as "The story of a man who could not make up his mind," the opening text of the 1948 Oscar-winning film version of *Hamlet.* However, the Professor is no Olivier: by hand-cranking his record player, he awakens Hecuba with the noise of the castaways' rehearsal of a musical.

The sequence of the actual performance of the musical *Hamlet* is made up of individual production numbers that poorly summarize the plot of the play. First, Gilligan as Hamlet sings "To be or not to be" to the tune of *Carmen.* Mr. and Mrs. Howell (Claudius and Gertrude) provide the harmony: "A rogue and peasant slave is he." Next, Hamlet hears Ophelia coming. Gilligan tells her to "get thee to a notarary [sic]," mixing up Shakespeare's nunn'ry (3.1.120) and a notary public. Ginger as Ophelia (to the tune of *Tales of Hoffmann*) gives Hamlet advice, reversing Shakespeare's scene: "Hamlet dear . . . you're content to try to catch the conscience of the King. . . . You hate your mom. . . . You'll kill the King or some such thing. . . . Leave the gravediggers' scene, if you know what I mean. Danish pastry for two. For me. For you." After listening to her sing, Hamlet tells Ophelia to "hide anyplace, but don't go near the water," an inside joke that requires a considerable knowledge of Shakespeare's *Hamlet* in order to follow along.

Finally, Polonius (the Skipper) gives advice to Laertes (Mary Ann as a boy). "Oh, could I tell him a few stories," says Laertes in aside to the camera, replicating the gender-bending play of an actual Shakespearean comedy. The Skipper sings "Neither a borrower nor a lender be," Polonius's advice to Laertes from act 1, scene 3, as the final number. The castaways join in refrain to the tune of *Carmen*. The narrative incoherence of the musical—adapting only material from the first few acts of *Hamlet*—makes the performance in "The Producer" one of the most radical audiovisual revisions in the Shakespearean canon. As the Ophelia and Laertes jokes indicate, however, this is not just an asinine butchering of *Hamlet*. By only focusing on the first few acts, the castaways successfully turn the tragedy into a comedy, at its most basic, the very theme of *Gilligan's Island* itself. What is brutally real on the mainland, the castaways convert into twenty-three-minute diversions, inviting us to "sit right back" and enjoy ourselves with the zany performances of seven stranded castaways whom we quickly come to love, even if not for their singing ability.

For his part, Hecuba loves the concept of the musical *Hamlet*. He takes over the production. Mirroring actual Hollywood producers, Hecuba threatens of Shakespeare: "If he was alive today, I'd have him working on a full re-write." The castaways continue to rehearse, but now that Hecuba is in charge, the impromptu fun of the performance for the castaways has been lost. Hecuba yells at the castaways, telling them how terrible they are. Hecuba jokes, "Up until now, there's really been something rotten in the state of Denmark." Hecuba observes that he will have to do the entire show himself. "An original production created by Harold Hecuba," the producer crows. Mr. Howell sneers ironically: "What a modest, unassuming chap." Coming from arrogant Mr. Howell, this is quite a potent observation. This is one of the central motifs of *Gilligan's Island*: despite the castaways' significant shortcomings, they are decent people,

The castaways perform the finale of *Hamlet: The Musical* in "The Producer" (October 3, 1966).

who do not seem capable of the real-world horrors occurring back on the mainland. There, real tycoons ruin the American economy, and real scientists devise more and more ghoulish ways to destroy the earth.

When Hecuba does the show alone, he outdoes even the castaways' performance. He tells the Professor he needs more pace; the Professor obliges by cranking the record player faster and faster. Hecuba sings Ginger's part in a wig and a dress. Every time he changes costume, he goes out the door at the back of the stage, and the entire image shakes, Schwartz's comic invention in the editing room after the Phil Silvers footage had already been shot. After enacting every role, Hecuba collapses. The castaways put him to bed, assured that they have hooked the producer on their idea, and that rescue is imminent.

Phil Silvers demonstrates how to play Ophelia in "The Producer" (October 3, 1966).

However, the next morning, Gilligan tells the Skipper that Hecuba is gone. The producer at least left a note: the rescue boat came in the middle of the night. The Professor brings the radio with the update that Hecuba has returned to the mainland and is doing the musical version of *Hamlet*: "Who but Harold Hecuba could come up with a brilliant idea like that?" enthuses the radio announcer. Gilligan shrugs at the inevitability of the castaways having their intellectual property stolen: "Well, that's show biz!" Once again, they will not be rescued. But, in their desperate attempt at rescue, they have taken the Shakespearean audiovisual adaptation to new creative heights.

Prospero's Children

Given *Gilligan's Island*'s interest in utopian literature, it is not the one-off episode riffing on *Hamlet* that establishes the full Shake-spearean force of Schwartz's show. Instead, *Gilligan's Island* is at its most Shakespearean in its engagement with the themes of the Bard's last play, *The Tempest* (1611), another important text about an American island community. The engagement with the newly colonized America is the source material that mo-tivates Shakespeare in his last play. As Leo Marx argues in his essay "Shakespeare's American Fable," *The Tempest* expresses the contradiction of the New World as being simultaneously a hell on earth and a new Garden of Eden, depending on which Englishman returning from the newly established Jamestown Colony, permanently founded in 1607, one read. Shakespeare creates a slippage between the island's location, narratively in the Mediterranean Sea (the noblemen in the play have em-barked on boats from Italy, and the shipwreck occurs shortly after their departure) and symbolically in the New World. Ariel tells Prospero early in the play:

> Safely in harbour
> Is the King's ship, in the deep nook where once
> Thou called'st me up at midnight to fetch dew
> From the still-vexed Bermudas, there she's hid. (1.2.226–29)

While *The Tempest* is concerned with shipwrecks within a transatlantic paradigm, Schwartz's twentieth-century *Tempest* is situated in the Pacific. His castaways flee a 1960s America, the corrupted civilization equivalent to Shakespeare's England and Italy. The events on *The Tempest*'s island and Schwartz's are remarkably similar. In Shakespeare, Prospero summons his corrupt relatives to punish them for their transgression against him. In dozens of episodes of *Gilligan's Island,* the vicissitudes of the Pacific Ocean currents float all sorts of ne'er-do-wells onto the island. In "The Hunter" (season 3, episode 86, January 16, 1967), a man comes to the island and wants to hunt Gilligan for sport. In another episode, gangsters come to hide their loot. In short, the plotting European schemers in *The Tempest,* Stephano and Trinculo, have their direct analogues in Schwartz's Pacific island cosmos.

Furthermore, the basic familial dynamics of *The Tempest* are replicated in *Gilligan's Island.* Prospero's paternal relationship to innocent Miranda is mimicked in the Professor and Skipper's protection of the virginal Mary Ann. The naïf Gilligan, the classical American Adam studied by R. W. B. Lewis and Leo Marx, is an asexual version of Caliban, Shakespeare's native islander. In *The American Adam,* Lewis argues that American exceptionalism is built on American culture's embrace of the European immigrant's new land and his escape from the corruption and confines of Europe. Lewis proposes that American literature celebrates the flourishing of an innocent (such as Huckleberry Finn) in a new land and laments the fall of those who lose their Adamic innocence (such as Jay Gatsby).

Classical American studies of the 1960s fully imbues *Gilligan's Island.* The show is a fellow traveler with Lewis and Marx, who argue for American exceptionalism via the well-meaning yet simple folks who populate our literary culture. While Marx begins *The Machine in the Garden* with the astonishing claim that *The Tempest* is the first piece of American literature, *Gilligan's Island* seems to cap the trajectory of that experience as its apotheosis, producing a renewed televised tempest at precisely the time Marx's book advances the academic cause of American studies.

The Tempest exists within a chain of Renaissance utopian philosophy. Within the play, the elderly counselor, Gonzalo, expresses the desire of Europeans to escape the Machiavellian corruption of their political lives. When first thinking about the island, Gonzalo delivers a paean to the possibilities of Utopia:

> I'th' commonwealth I would by contraries Execute all things, for no kind of traffic
> Would I admit; no name of magistrate; Letters should not be

known; riches, poverty
And use of service, none; contract, succession,
Bourn, bound of land, tilth, vineyard, none;
No use of metal, corn, or wine, or oil;
No occupation, all men idle, all,
And women too, but innocent and pure; no sovereignty.
(2.1.145–54)

Yet undermining this vision are characters, both powerful (Alonso and Sebastian) and comic (Stefano and Trinculo), who only have their own petty interests at heart.

Many *Gilligan's Island* episodes are built around the very same constraint on the possibility of utopia. The steady state of the series is utopian: the castaways live off the resources of the island. It is only the narrative demand for drama, to produce the temporary conflicts of the twenty-three-minute episodes, which intrudes on the utopian experience. In episode after episode, a scheme arises that shakes the castaways out of Gonzalo's utopian reverie. Someone questions who is the most beautiful woman on the island, thus pitting the men and women against each other. A radio report informs the castaways that one among their number is a murderer. In "Gilligan Goes Gung-Ho," the castaways live peacefully until a law book washes up on shore. The castaways become convinced that they are imminently going to become the victims of crime, despite the fact that they have been living peacefully without incident for three years. Once a botched election for sheriff places Gilligan in charge, the young lad sees crime in every castaway's behavior, resulting in the arrest in short order of all six castaways.

In no episode is the Shakespearean disruption of the utopian more prominent than in "President Gilligan" (season 1, episode 6, October 31, 1964). To survive, the Professor and the Skipper are digging a well. The Professor wants Gilligan to help dig, but the Howells have the lad building their private estate. The Skipper and Mr. Howell fight over Gilligan's labor.

Gilligan guards his cave jail in "Gilligan Goes Gung-Ho" (December 26, 1966).

The Skipper says that as captain of the boat, he is in charge of the island. As a business tycoon, Mr. Howell insists that he is the chairman of the board and therefore outranks the Skipper. A scientist, the Professor observes that no one is in charge of the island. To resolve the conflict democratically, Ginger comes up with the idea of having an election for president.

In act 1, each of the candidates, the Skipper and Mr. Howell, behave as corruptly as did their Shakespearean predecessors, Alonso and Sebastian, who schemed to exile Prospero from Italy, and Stephano and Trinculo, who plot with Caliban to murder Prospero when on the island. Mr. Howell tries to bribe Mary Ann and Ginger, to woo their votes. He tells Ginger that he will buy Hollywood for her. Then, Ginger, working for Mr. Howell, goes to seduce Gilligan. She tries to kiss him, but the naïf is unprepared for her sexuality: he knocks himself out against a tree. She looks into the camera and shrugs. Mr.

Howell then tries to bribe Gilligan by promising to make him secretary of the navy.

In an uncanny prediction of *Survivor* (CBS, 2000–present)—yet in a utopian way that sociologically binds us rather than divides us—the Professor invents an election booth on the primitive island. The Professor counts the votes: two votes for Mr. Howell (Ginger and Mr. Howell) and two votes for Skipper (Skipper and Gilligan). There is a write-in vote for Gilligan by Mrs. Howell, and then another for Gilligan from Mary Ann. The third vote is for Gilligan! Act 2 thus begins with Gilligan having been elected president because scheming and bribery backfired against Mr. Howell and the Skipper. But not having learned his lesson, Mr. Howell again comes to bribe Gilligan. The Skipper also has learned nothing, insisting he is the vice president because of his close relationship with his little buddy. Mr. Howell appoints himself chief justice of the Supreme Court because he has been arrested six times for antitrust violations.

For his part, Gilligan tries his best as the new leader. He gives a speech during dinner, insisting that they pitch in to dig a well. But Gilligan has no real authority; they all ignore him. Throughout the rest of the episode, Gilligan tries to get the well dug. He again tries to get the Skipper to pay attention to their survival needs, but the greedy sailor is more interested in a new hut that befits a vice president.

Finally, Gilligan takes the government into his own hands. He digs the well himself as the others stand and argue. Refusing to grant Gilligan any authority whatsoever, none of the castaways believe there is any water there. Gilligan quits. As he drives his shovel into the hole in disgust, he hits water. The episode's coda returns the narrative to the status quo: Gilligan has a new rescue plan; he proposes that they build a lookout tower to spot passing ships. However, all the other castaways make excuses not to help him.

Unlike *Gilligan's Island,* Shakespeare's *The Tempest* begins with tragedy looming. Prospero summons the tempest in order that his enemies stand before him to face his judgment. However, because of the comic masque in act 4 celebrating the marriage of Prospero's daughter, Miranda, to Alonso's son, Ferdinand, the familial bonds heal the wounds of the past. *The Tempest* ends comically, with the schemes diffused of danger and all setting sail to return to Italy. So, too, does *Gilligan's Island* diffuse real danger. Whenever a nefarious visitor arrives on the island, Gilligan, through luck or pluck, wins the day. When the hunter after human game is about to shoot Gilligan, the boy hides in a tree trunk, comically moving the object out of the rifle sights each time it is aimed at his heart. Just as Gilligan is about to be killed, the hunter's watch timer goes off, indicating that Gilligan has won the battle between predator and prey.

In short, *Gilligan's Island* is one of the most Shakespearean

Rory Calhoun tracks Gilligan in "The Hunter" (January 16, 1967).

texts in the history of American television. While Shakespearean scholars have rightly emphasized the wonders of the musical version of *Hamlet* in the episode "The Producer," it is my belief that the more pressing Shakespearean intertext, because of its engagement with an American island utopia, is *The Tempest*.

A Poke in CBS's Eye: The Aesthetics of *Gilligan's Island*

In his foundational study of the history of comedy, Northrop Frye discusses the green world of Shakespearean comedy, such as the forest in *A Midsummer Night's Dream* (1596), that space to which characters retreat to avoid the seriousness of the world and from which they emerge cleansed to take up their duties in their rightful adult places. This shift from the tragedy of *Hamlet* to the comic romance of *The Tempest* in Shakespeare scholarship is a recapitulation of my project on *Gilligan's Island,* nudging the focus from the serious issues of the 1960s and its television (everything from the coverage of the Kennedy assassination to *The Fugitive* [ABC, 1963–67]) to the wasteland sitcoms such as *Bewitched, Gilligan's Island,* and *The Beverly Hillbillies.* In short, the jungle of *Gilligan's Island* is an important green world in American television, a 1960s space of retreat that duels with corporate industry.

Indeed, the key aesthetic element of *Gilligan's Island,* its Robinson Crusoe-cum-Rube Goldberg island contraptions, represent an assault on the industrial design of the network on which the show appeared. As Lynn Spigel details, CBS built its network brand in the 1950s and 1960s on its sleek, modern design. In *TV by Design: Modern Art and the Rise of Network Television,* Spigel studies the building of CBS into a visually coherent enterprise of modernity, from graphic designer William

Golden's "eye" (to this day, CBS's global corporate logo), to the commissioning of modernist photographer Paul Strand to help brand the company in the early 1950s.

Unlike the sleek interior design of *The Dick Van Dyke Show,* including the square ottoman that Rob Petrie trips over in that show's credit sequence, *Gilligan's Island* embraced an aesthetic of antimodernist primitivism. This may in fact be the reason why the show was canceled, despite being very highly rated. Unlike *Gunsmoke,* which took over *Gilligan's Island*'s time slot, Schwartz's show deliberately parodied the consumerism of postwar American modernity. While set in the nineteenth century, *Gunsmoke* nevertheless highlighted objects (such as metallic guns and marshal's stars) and wooden sets that could replicate the clean lines of CBS iconography.

Such collisions were common in the art world of postwar America. As Spigel argues, "One of the defining features of midcentury modernism is the continuum between modern (fine) art and everyday objects (often designed in mass-produced knock-offs for middleclass consumers)" (11). With its bamboo roughness and kludgy jungle vines holding its props together, *Gilligan's Island* drove its handmade thatch car (one of the most beloved objects remembered from the show) off the midcentury modernist continuum into the realm of surrealist cartoon comedy.

Such a gesture was an aesthetic assault to the CBS brand. As Spigel defines that brand, "One of the network's primary goals was to promote consumerism, their success in this regard depended largely on their liaisons with the visual arts and modern design (in both commercial and museum contexts)" (9). *Gilligan's Island* conversely retreated from mainland consumerism, parodying the objects otherwise celebrated by "the Tiffany Network." While other 1960s CBS shows grappled with nonurban lifestyles, most of those "barnyard sitcoms" remained within the midcentury modernist continuum. *The Beverly Hillbillies*' characters came from middle America, but their milieu within the

Gilligan drives a bamboo car while CBS tries to sell new, sleek, metallic models in "The Producer" (October 3, 1966).

show featured the devices of modern living. *Green Acres* (CBS, 1965–71) offered a similar hybridity, purporting to retreat into the American heartland but nevertheless narratively clinging to the urban milieu of the network and the sponsors (especially via the hysterical attachment Lisa Douglas [Eva Gabor] felt toward that world).

Thus, even legendary television creator Paul Henning's famous barnyard CBS sitcoms—*The Beverly Hillbillies, Petticoat Junction* (1963–70), and *Green Acres*—famous for their rural settings, fell short of embracing the comic green world. On the other hand, *Gilligan's Island* aesthetically documents the absurdity of midcentury modernism. The car that the Professor builds, and Gilligan drives, is completely unnecessary on the island. The only object that remains from postwar consumerist

America is the radio, which cloyingly connects the castaways to the mainland, yet never helps them find a way back. It is the parody contraptions, not the radio or the abandoned ship, which dominate the visual aesthetic of *Gilligan's Island*. To do laundry, the Professor builds a bamboo washing machine, but like its midcentury modernist equivalent back on the mainland, the device causes as much work as it saves: Gilligan must pedal like a lunatic for the machine to work. In short, the green world of *Gilligan's Island* offers a direct assault on CBS corporate branding, even more aggressively than the rural sitcoms that surround it.

Gilligan Goes to Carnival

Ever since 1960s telefilm sitcoms entered incredibly success-ful syndication on early morning and late afternoon local television stations, they have been much reviled for their ap-peal to children. Indeed, I fell in love with *Gilligan's Island* as a child watching after school syndicated reruns day after day in the 1970s on Boston UHF channels. These exhibition con-texts cloud the status of *Gilligan's Island* as a virtual textbook of comedy in the Western tradition. Indeed, early in "St. Gilligan and the Dragon," Mrs. Howell invites Ginger and Mary Ann to move across the island by invoking Aristophanes's *Lysistrata* (411 BCE). Explaining that the Greek women engineered a sex strike to stop the Peloponnesian War, Mrs. Howell convinces the women to build their own hut.

Most important, Gilligan and the Skipper continue a tradi-tion of partner comedy from vaudeville to Hollywood to the television sitcom. Most obviously, Gilligan and Skipper replay Laurel and Hardy, an earlier comedy duo consisting of a thin guy who annoys his portly compatriot. Vaudeville and silent cinema traditions would become staples of the television sit-com, from Ralph Kramden and Ed Norton on *The Honeymoon-*

ers (CBS, 1950–51) to Jerry Seinfeld and George Costanza on *Seinfeld.*

However, I believe there is a deeper significance to the comedy in *Gilligan's Island.* In *Rabelais and His World,* Mikhail Bakhtin argues that medieval carnival served as a kind of safety valve for Western civilization in which a celebration of the lower bodily strata of human bodies temporarily overturned the normally oppressive social hierarchy. A literary scholar, Bakhtin argues that the radical tradition of carnival continued in literature, through François Rabelais's series of sixteenth-century novels about the giants Gargantua and Pantagruel. Contemporary media scholars have seen such carnivalesque interventions in the American sitcom. Kathleen Rowe, for example, argues that Roseanne Barr is a carnivalesque figure whose overweight body produces a similar celebration of the lower bodily strata to Rabelais's novels.

At first glance, *Gilligan's Island* seems the complete opposite of the carnivalesque. When Schwartz discusses his show in his many books and interviews, he celebrates its clean storytelling. With pride, in the commentary track to "The Producer" on the recently released DVD set, Schwartz proclaims that his show was never blue, dirty, or racy. Thus, there is very little scatological grotesquery on *Gilligan's Island.* However, several episodes of *Gilligan's Island* feature Rabelaisian comedy open to Bakhtinian cultural analysis.

The most significant episode in this regard is "Pass the Vegetables, Please" (season 3, episode 71, September 26, 1966) in which Gilligan fishes a box of radioactive seeds out of the Pacific Ocean. Since he makes the box, which is labeled "Danger, Experimental Radio Active Seeds," into a stool, the castaways do not know the seeds are contaminated. Delighted to be able to grow vegetables for the first time on the island, Skipper, Gilligan, Mary Ann, and the Professor plant the seeds in a garden. In three days' time, the vegetable plants grow to gargantuan proportions. Mary Ann harvests a huge, four-pronged carrot,

The Skipper dons a "budget corn" necklace in "Pass the Vegetables, Please" (September 26, 1966).

which she jokes is the size of a cow udder. The cucumbers are a yard long. Skipper jokes that the corn, which has grown so long as to circle back on itself, must be "budget corn—it makes both ends meet."

The castaways sit down to a huge, carnivalesque feast. They consume the vegetables with delight. When each castaway cannot reach the serving plate containing their favorites quickly enough, the Professor suggests that they move the plate right next to them to facilitate quicker gorging. However, in the middle of the meal, the radio announces a story about radioactive seeds that were lost at sea in the Pacific Ocean. Gilligan shows the Professor the stool he made out of the seed crate, thus putting a damper on the castaways' bacchanalia.

The seeds have a comic effect on the castaways. Gilligan's love of spinach has resulted in superhuman strength (he gently tosses a coconut to the Skipper, but it destroys the hut, traveling at the speed of a bullet); Mary Ann has extraordinary eyesight due to consumption of her favorite carrots (she sees a yacht miles away and thus of no help to getting them rescued); and Mrs. Howell cleans her hut in comically fast motion with the energy given to her by her beloved sugar beets. However, with these superhuman skills comes the news that they will die from radiation sickness. With the news that they have been poisoned, the castaways lie around waiting for the end. Suddenly, the Professor returns from his book research to tell them that they have to move around in order to expunge the radiation. He berates himself for being so stupid as to allow slothful lounging while in the midst of radiation sickness.

After more research, the Professor finds a cure. The castaways must consume plant fats to counteract the radioactivity. The only available source of the fats is from the soap they have been making from the island's plants, which they now have to eat. In one of the funniest, much-beloved visual moments in the show, the castaways sit around their dining table chewing on soap. When the characters talk, they spew not only words but also bubbles. In production, a bubble machine was housed behind each character's head, so that the set filled with bubbles. In a delightful ending, the castaways sitting around having a meal of soap cures them. The Professor shouts, "It's working! The hydrocarbons are absorbing the radioactivity!" In the episode's coda, Gilligan and the Skipper lie in the hammocks that night. Even though cured, Gilligan is still eating the soap in bed. He blows a huge bubble after swallowing a huge chunk of soap. The bubble explodes all over the Skipper as the end credits roll.

This episode is intriguingly Bakhtinian in its logic. As with medieval carnival, the castaways hold a bacchanalian feast and gorge themselves on the vegetables, as rare a meal on the tropical island as the medieval feasts of meat and drink would have been to the villagers. However, the gorging itself is not a problem within the episode. Instead, it is the technological ad-

The castaways exhale radioactive bubbles in "Pass the Vegetables, Please" (September 26, 1966).

vancement of the modern world—the development of radioactive seeds—that poisons them, not their gluttony. The solution to this radioactive assault on humanity is, remarkably, another bacchanalia. In a delightful celebration of community at the end of the episode, the castaways sit down for a family meal to consume the soap. Their bodily excess literally carries away the poisonous hydrocarbons into the air. The laughter of carnival, both of the castaways and the audience, is the cure to modern technology's poisoning of the environment. While not strictly about the lower bodily strata as are the novels about Gargantua and Pantagruel, this is the liberating politics of the carnivalesque that Bakhtin sees as the cornerstone of our response to the terrors of early modernity.

Gilligan and the Short Story

While *The Tempest* is clearly the urtext behind the premise of *Gilligan's Island,* series television is based on a need to, in individual episodes, reinvent the basic premise in unusual ways. Exposing itself to critical ridicule, *Gilligan's Island* achieved this reinvention by absurdly having an endless number of objects and people wash up on the shore of the island to generate a new plot for the week. A literate show, *Gilligan's Island* featured a number of episodes that adapted famous short stories in interesting ways. For example, "The Hunter" is an adaptation of Richard Connell's "The Most Dangerous Game" (1924).

As the episode opens, Gilligan listens to the radio as a helicopter lands on the island. Beside himself with excitement, Gilligan crashes into Jonathan Kincaid, the hunter, who asks our little buddy if there is game on the island. Confused, Gilligan says there are no wild animals of which he is aware. When Gilligan runs off to tell the other castaways about their imminent rescue, Kincaid tells his servant Ramu that he has found the ultimate hunting experience: "I've always wondered what it would feel like to track the most interesting game, Man."

When Kincaid announces to the castaways that he is planning on hunting one of them, innocent Mary Ann replies, "That's ridiculous. People don't hunt people." Kincaid will not change his mind. After much deliberation about who his quarry will be—"I'd love to let some hot air out of your stuffed shirt," he says of Mr. Howell—he decides on Gilligan because he is the most nimble and most attuned to the animals on the island.

All of the castaways do their part to try to talk Kincaid out of hunting Gilligan. In the show's conventional act 2 sequence, all the castaways take a turn at changing the direction of the plot. Ginger comes to seduce Kincaid. She offers him a toast, poisoning his glass of pineapple juice. But when he puts down his glass, Gilligan drinks it and passes out. For his part, Mr. Howell tries to bribe Kincaid not to hunt Gilligan. Kincaid says that he is not interested in money. "You are sick," says Mr. Howell. What is usually a joke on *Gilligan's Island*—Mr. Howell's love of money over people—is now deadly serious. While refusing to call off the hunt for Gilligan, Kincaid does make a deal with the castaways: if the hunted can elude him for twenty-four hours, he will see to it that they are returned to civilization.

The next morning, Kincaid tells Gilligan the rules and sets his watch. He gives Gilligan a fifteen-minute head start. The lad runs right out of his shoes, but his slapstick comedy is not well designed for eluding a professional big-game hunter. Gilligan tries to keep running, but he is already dead tired, having only been running for five minutes. However, nature is on the side of Gilligan. Gilligan sits down to rest. He talks to an owl. Kincaid shoots at Gilligan, but the boy bends down just as the shot rings out. A little later, Gilligan falls into a fresh water trough. Gilligan pulls Kincaid into the trough, running away. Kincaid fires his gun at him, but it is filled with water and does not work.

The Professor and Skipper hide Gilligan in a hollow tree trunk. However, Kincaid finally has Gilligan cornered. The castaways try one last desperate time to talk Kincaid out of pulling the trigger. Gilligan turns the target away from Kincaid and comically moves his tree back and forth away from Kincaid's aim. Gilligan's shenanigans have paid off: just as Kincaid is about to fire, his twenty-four-hour alarm goes off. Kincaid agrees not to shoot Gilligan, but once again the castaways are not rescued. Kincaid cannot fulfill his end of the bargain because the authorities would put him in jail if the castaways ever returned to the mainland with their story of his hunting humans. However, Gilligan and his infuriatingly simple nature win in the end. During the coda to the episode, the announcer on the radio informs the castaways that Kincaid won a national shooting competition, hitting one hundred clay pigeons in a row. However, they had to put the winner in a straitjacket and banish him to a mental institution: during the competition, all he kept muttering was "Gilligan!"

Gilligan's Island and Film History

Along with other 1960s telefilm sitcoms such as *Bewitched*, *Gilligan's Island* gave directorial work both to classical Hollywood directors (such as Jack Arnold, who had directed Russell Johnson in 1950s science fiction films) and to young up-and-coming directors such as Richard Donner (who would go on to direct 1978's *Superman* and the *Lethal Weapon* films). Perhaps most intriguingly, film studies' recent rediscovery of Ida Lupino as one of the few women directors from the classical Hollywood period has turned attention to *Gilligan's Island,* of which she directed six episodes.

63

Despite auteurist critics' rescue project to uncover Lupino's role behind the cameras in Hollywood, these same critics reject her work in television situation comedy in almost identical ways to the original erasure of her film directing. In their entry on Lupino in *The Encyclopedia of Television,* Mary Celeste Kearney and James Moran explain, "Although she directed episodes of *The Untouchables* and *The Fugitive,* whose intricate weekly subplots and relatively large guest casts required her creative input, her influence on formulaic series such as *Gilligan's Island* or *Bewitched* was minimal" (1390). Similarly, in *Disaster and Memory: Celebrity Culture and the Crisis of Hollywood Cinema,* Wheeler Winston Dixon argues, "There is little to say, for example, about Lupino's work on *Bewitched* or *Gilligan's Island,* but her work for *The Untouchables* and *Thriller* is often adventurous and individualistic" (71).

I believe, in fact, there is quite a lot to say about Lupino and *Gilligan's Island.* For one thing, while the role of the director in episodic television is significantly different than in feature filmmaking (the "creative control" sometimes given to a film director is often in the hands of a television producer, as it was in the case of Schwartz and *Gilligan's Island*), it is nonetheless the case that the television director is fully in charge of orchestrating the filming of the dramatic scenes on set and getting the best performances possible out of his or her actors, just as in film direction. Lupino orchestrated the image and got wonderful performances out of her actors, both in the feature films she directed, such as *The Bigamist* (1953), and in her situation comedy work.

The episodes of *Gilligan's Island* that Lupino directed are remarkable for a number of reasons. For one thing, Lupino helmed early first season episodes—the fourth, "Goodnight, Sweet Skipper" (October 17, 1964) and the fifth, "Wrongway Feldman" (October 24, 1964)—at precisely the time the show was shifting from its opening episodes' *serial* establishment of the characters' given circumstances on the island to an episodic *series* format. In "Goodnight, Sweet Skipper," the trauma suffered by the Skipper during World War II is plumbed for dramatic effect and foregrounds Alan Hale Jr.'s skill as a dramatic, in addition to comedic, actor.

The next episode, "Wrongway Feldman," is the first episode of *Gilligan's Island* to feature a guest star, a format that the show would use to great effect later on, as in the well-remembered episode "The Producer," featuring Phil Silvers as the producer of a musical version of *Hamlet*, a third-season episode also codirected by Ida Lupino. In "Wrongway Feldman," Hans Conreid portrays a flying ace who has accidentally landed his airplane on the island. Conreid, a well-known character actor from the classical Hollywood cinema (his first film was 1938's *Dramatic School*) found himself in the 1960s in similar circumstances to Lupino, bouncing around between film and television, taking small jobs as they came.

As Dixon admits, "Most previous studies of Lupino have failed to consider her television work, yet a careful examination of her series projects reveals that her directorial sensibility is still apparent, although muted, to some degree by the inevitable television treadmill" (71). This motivates an intervention into the significance television studies can have for the well-studied area of auteurist film theory. Since the foundations of the discipline, articulated by Andrew Sarris in *The American Cinema* (1968), authorship theory has posited the notion that a film director's oeuvre coalesces certain stylistic practices and themes, for example, audio innovations and questioning the human capacity for evil in the case of Orson Welles. The rescue operation on Ida Lupino staged a critique of the sexism of authorship theory in previously only positing great white men as the controllers of great films' meaning.

65

In this corrective, inclusionary logic, *The Bigamist* is also a great film because Lupino applies the traditions of the film noir to a study of the implications of crime on the lives of women. In the film, an adoption agency official, Mr. Jordan (Edmund Gwenn), uses his detective skills to unearth the fact that a seemingly wholesome man, Harry Graham (Edmond O'Brien), who lives with his wife, Eve (Joan Fontaine), in San Francisco is also keeping another wife, Phyllis (Ida Lupino), in Los Angeles. In a wonderful use of film noir flashback narration, Harry explains how he succumbed to temptation in Los Angeles, falling in love with Phyllis while on a tour of the stars' houses.

The complexity of *The Bigamist*—relying on a shift between two levels of narration, that about Harry falling in love with two women, and that about the star power of Ida Lupino and Los Angeles—indeed makes the film worthy of auteurist study. However, if we agree with the poststructural critique of such auteurism that the collaborative nature of audiovisual production means that many complex forces come together in the creation of the artwork, then the coherency of Lupino's work can be seen as relating not just to her particular duties while directing *The Bigamist* or an episode of *Gilligan's Island* but to the cultural complexity of film and television production itself, what both André Bazin and Thomas Schatz refer to as "the genius of the system." In Michel Foucault's terms, we should properly seek to analyze Ida Lupino's "author function" in Hollywood filmmaking and 1960s television production.

Through this prism, it is possible to trace the expression of Lupino themes familiar from *The Bigamist* within the *Gilligan's Island* episodes she directed. For, like *The Bigamist,* "The Producer" concerns the immorality of show business practitioners. Harold Hecuba shows no compunction about stealing the castaways' intellectual property and premiering "his" musical version of *Hamlet* on Broadway and refusing to tell the authorities about the existence of the castaways on the desert island to cover up his sin. As in *The Bigamist,* in which Los Angeles symbolically expresses the site of immorality, so too in *Gilligan's Island* does the mainland serve as an immoral contrast to the utopian dynamics of the island. The actual duties of Lupino on the set of the episode have little to do with this argument. It is impossible to trace what scenes Lupino shot, as Cahan replaced her when she became injured and could not continue work on the episode.

Thus, the production history of *Gilligan's Island* alone indicates the show's complex relationship to Hollywood. Beyond this, in its intertextual referencing, *Gilligan's Island* obsesses over popular cinema and film history more generally. Gilligan has seen every movie Ginger Grant ever made, who in turn is a simulacrum of Marilyn Monroe. The Professor does a killer impersonation of Cary Grant: "Judy, Judy, Judy," the high school teacher enthuses when he wants to pitch woo to Ginger.

There are two remarkable episodes that engage with the cinema as an art form as well. As previously discussed, in "Diogenes, Won't You Please Go Home?," the plot interrogates the castaways' memories of a prior episode in which a Japanese sailor attacked the castaways, thinking World War II was still going on. The episode embraces the modernism of *Rashomon* in order to query the relationship between truth and memory. In the second, "Castaways Pictures Presents," Gilligan fishes a crate containing silent film equipment out of the ocean. The castaways make a silent movie intended to indicate to those on the mainland their location. However, the castaways' bickering during production causes the film to be so obtuse as to be mistaken by those who find it as a lost masterpiece collaborated on by Ingmar Bergman and Vittorio De Sica. The film easily wins the grand prize at the Cannes Film Festival but does not cause the castaways to be rescued.

"Diogenes, Won't You Please Go Home?" concerns a diary that Gilligan has begun writing. The other castaways become obsessed with the content of Gilligan's diary, assuming that he

Bicyclist Gilligan powers the projector as the castaways finish watching their experimental film in "Castaways Pictures Presents" (11/4/65)

has documented their frailties. In the middle of the episode, Gilligan whittles using the bayonet he took from the Japanese soldier's rifle. Gilligan tells Mrs. Howell that he has only been writing the truth in his diary. Gilligan tells her that he wishes all the castaways would write their own journals, so that they would be less obsessed with his. The Skipper takes Gilligan up on this suggestion. Gilligan whittles away with the bayonet while Skipper is trying to write, annoying him yet again. The Skipper takes the bayonet from Gilligan, who reminds the Skipper that Gilligan rescued the castaways from the Japanese soldier. In a flashback, we witness Gilligan's version of the events in which he bravely steals the key to the cells where the soldier is holding the castaways.

Skipper responds incredulously: "Gilligan, I have never heard a weirder fabrication." Skipper says that if it were not for him, Gilligan would not be here at all. The Skipper reads from his diary. A flashback ensues in which the Skipper is the great hero. The terrible acting highlighted in the flashback reveals the inaccuracy of the Skipper's story. Skipper holds a live hand grenade in order to protect the women from the explosion. Skipper's version is a tall tale: he rips apart the soldier's machine gun with his bare hands.

Gilligan then goes to Mr. Howell to tell him about the Skipper's odd version of the story. Mr. Howell reads to Gilligan his version of the story. Mr. Howell insists he tricked the Japanese soldier into locking him inside the cell. Like a true adventurer, Mr. Howell uses his whip to grab the soldier's rifle just as he is about to execute Gilligan. Mr. Howell insists, "I'm sure you remember now." Gilligan observes that the Skipper's and Mr. Howell's stories do not agree at all.

Gilligan then goes to talk to Ginger, who also has a version of the story in which she is the hero of the experience with the Japanese soldier. In Ginger's version she is a judo expert who knocks out the soldier in a fight. Mary Ann finds Gilligan's diary. She reads the diary to the other characters. He says incredibly nice things about each castaway. Gilligan comes to ask if the castaways are still mad at him. They treat him so well, Gilligan insists it must be a dream. Later that night, all the castaways burn their diaries. When Gilligan tries to burn his, they stop him. The Professor explains: "We see us as we are, and you see us as we would like to be." The episode thus captures the two major qualities of *Rashomon*. First, it is a modernist interrogation of narrative and truth. In both the film and the episode, each version of the story cannot be the truth, since the personal interests of the storyteller infect each story.

Second, both texts end with a humanist affirmation. In *Rashomon,* the man has his faith in humankind restored as the poor father agrees to take care of the baby, since one more mouth to feed will not make any difference to him. The Professor also has his faith in the world restored, observing that Gilligan is a true friend because he sees the good in the castaways, rather than the petty jealousy of which they are so guilty. In short, the Professor has his Diogenes-like cynicism stripped away by Gilligan's utopian vision of the castaways.

Gilligan's Island's metaphoric reworking of the modernist storytelling of *Rashomon* is matched by the show's interest in film history in the episode "Castaway Pictures Presents." The Skipper finds a sunken ship in the lagoon filled with boxes containing silent film equipment. Immediately, the castaways try on the costumes from the filmmaking materials belonging to South Seas Film Productions. Ginger dresses like Theda Bara, Mary Ann like Mary Pickford, and Gilligan like Charlie Chaplin, thus establishing that the character types represented by the cast of *Gilligan's Island* have long-standing precedents in Hollywood film history.

For his part, the Professor has an idea of how to use the equipment to get rescued: the castaways will make a film and float it into the shipping lanes. Mr. Howell directs the film while the Professor runs the camera. The filming proves disastrous. On-screen, the Professor wants to shake hands with Ginger, but Mr. Howell insists that they kiss. Unfamiliar with movie romance, the Professor turns his head when Ginger tries to kiss him. Ever the scientist, he asserts that kissing is not sanitary. Ginger amorously throws the Professor over the table. Gilligan walks in front of the camera, mesmerized by the movie-making process, ruining the shot.

In a perverse recapitulation of the plots of *Gilligan's Island* episodes, Mary Ann is in a scene to show the everyday dangers on the island. Gilligan is an islander who captures Mary Ann. Gilligan ties her to a stake. Gilligan gets dizzy running around the stake. Mr. Howell is again frustrated: "Method actors. I tell you. Never again," he mumbles.

The Skipper tries to draw a map showing the approximate location of the island. The castaways argue over the point of reference on the mainland: Mr. Howell prefers Fort Knox, Ginger favors Hollywood. Mrs. Howell stands in front of the map, mugging to say hello on camera to Princess Grace. The other castaways similarly ruin the shot with their selfish attempts to upstage one another.

As act 3 of the episode begins, the castaways gather for the premiere of the film. As usual, the Professor had trouble with Gilligan bothering him while he was developing the film. The first shot is of a diary: "This is our story. . . . Help!" Like a Hollywood producer, Mr. Howell grumbles, "Message pictures don't make any money." In the next shot, Skipper rescues Ginger and Gilligan during the shipwreck scene. However, this shot is upside down. The film runs in reverse and shots are repeated, as if in a Sam Peckinpah action sequence: every time the Skipper throws Gilligan into the water, he jumps out again. Ginger's kiss with the Professor is played first in slow and then fast motion. Gilligan has shot an entire section in close-ups: we see the Professor's face in extreme close-up, complete with grotesque images of his lips and ears.

In short, the castaways have made an experimental film. Gilligan ruined much of the film, sticking his hand in front of the lens and opening the door to the darkroom during processing, resulting in shots of Gilligan and Mary Ann in reverse image. The finale of the movie conveys no information to the viewer about their whereabouts: there are too many castaways in the image and the film's spectator cannot see the map. The castaways all hate the movie. However, out of desperation, they seal it up tight and place it on a raft.

In the episode's coda, the radio reports that their film was discovered and is now beloved, especially the "blacked out" scenes. Film scholars think it is a lost Ingmar Bergman or Vittorio De Sica work. The announcer enthuses, "This ultra-modern version of Surrealism will bring back silent pictures." In this way, *Gilligan's Island* imports the traditions of international art cinema to popular American audiences in the most unlikely of vessels, the 1960s telefilm sitcom.

Gilligan's Island
and Performativity

These episodes about putting on a show (almost one-third of the entire run of the series, some thirty installments in all) serve as the innovative heart of *Gilligan's Island*. From the Shakespeare show, "The Producer," to the Broadway episodes ("Angel on the Island") to the dream sequences that allowed the cast to take on new roles in parodies of *High Noon* ("The Sound of Quacking"), *Dracula* ("Up at Bat"), and *Cinderella* ("Lovey's Secret Admirer"), *Gilligan's Island* represented to America that the defining feature of its microcosm of characters was that they performed for one another, both for ill (trying to trick one another into getting what they want) and as testament to the best people can be (protecting one another from threatening interlopers). These impulses allow me to theoretically trap the show between two influential, yet different, theories of performativity. On the one hand, the show was made well after the publication of Erving Goffman's *The Presentation of Self in Everyday Life* (1959), a crucial postwar sociological study of how and why people in professional and personal settings define their selves via what Goffman calls "theatrical performance." The fact that the book's research was based largely on Goffman's dissertation about a different set of islanders, the subsistence farmers of the Shetland Islands, is a source of karmic delight.

In the contemporary humanities, the most pervasive theories of the performative come from poststructural work, particularly that of Judith Butler. In her seminal work, *Gender Trouble: Feminism and the Subversion of Identity*—as well as her later studies, such as *Excitable Speech: A Politics of the Performative*—Butler intensifies the political implications of Goffman's work, arguing that key identity positions, such as gender and sex, are performative. Of course, *Gilligan's Island* was made well before poststructural theory, and I am not arguing that Sherwood Schwartz was reworking Goffman's sociological understanding of human behavior. Instead, I want to forward the notion that American television can be profitably understood as a representation machine in which actors are presented to the public as models for who and how to be. The best theoretical models for understanding this phenomenon lie in both historical (Goffman) and contemporary (Butler) theoretical explorations of the nature of performance and identity. While many other sitcoms come more immediately to mind concerning performance (from *I Love Lucy* to *Seinfeld*), *Gilligan's Island* is perhaps the most fertile because, while the show was not explicitly about performers, it ended up defining its seven castaways as exemplars of the lifestyle of radical performativity.

In virtually every episode of *Gilligan's Island,* performance is a central narrative concern. I will build a theoretical method for analyzing *Gilligan's Island* as a show that foregrounds performativity as a central human trait. In many of the most beloved episodes, the castaways put on a show. This is the case with "The Producer" in which Harold Hecuba steals their idea of a musical version of *Hamlet*. As another example, "Angel on the Island" is the first of many such episodes in which the castaways put on a play on their makeshift stage made of bamboo and adorned with a curtain patched together out of rags.

Even before the central plot of the episode begins, the castaways are engaged in their daily performative rituals. Gilligan tests a coconut telephone with Skipper, yet they are only three feet apart. When Mary Ann worries about Ginger, who has been missing all morning, the Skipper and Gilligan search the island. The Skipper suggests splitting up, but directionless Gilligan keeps crashing into him in an effort to go his separate way. The Skipper looks into the camera, exasperated, a populist reduction of a Brechtian direct address to the camera, coupled with the force of American film comedy (ranging from Oliver Hardy's exasperated looks to us about Stan Laurel to George Burns's quips to us about Gracie Allen in his groundbreaking early sitcom, *The George Burns and Gracie Allen Show* [CBS, 1950–58]).

Gilligan finally finds Ginger, who is crying while reading a script. This day was supposed to be her opening performance on Broadway, in a piece especially written for her. In a typically innocent joke, Gilligan expresses the central theme of *Gilligan's Island,* and of Erving Goffman, that real life is a performance: "You know what? You ought to be on the stage."

Later, Gilligan reads the play, performing it for Skipper's amusement. Mr. Howell wanders by and stops what he thinks is Gilligan's mutiny against the Skipper. When Mr. Howell comes to understand that they are rehearsing a play, *Pyramid for Two,* the millionaire agrees to put the full force of his fortune behind the enterprise, serving as the "angel" of the production. Despite the plot circumstances up until this point, the slippage between performance and real life continues to drive the episode's comedy. While Ginger rehearses, she exclaims, "A ship, I see a ship." Gilligan gets excited and thinks they are going to be rescued. Even when they are well into production, building the scenery for the stage, Gilligan is still confused about the boundary between the fictional and the real. Ginger as Cleopatra again rehearses the line "I see a ship." Gilligan runs onstage, excited, interrupting everything, again thinking they will be rescued.

Human pettiness drives the plot of the episode. Mrs. Howell asks for a private audience with the producer, her husband. She does not like her small part in the play; she instead wants to play Cleopatra. Mr. Howell foolishly capitulates, announcing that Mrs. Howell will be Cleopatra and Ginger will play the part of the maid.

As act 2 begins, Mrs. Howell now plays Cleopatra. "A ship," she enthuses. Gilligan yet again runs onto the stage. He is getting better, though. When everyone looks at him, annoyed, he observes, "Oh, still the play, huh?" But Mr. Howell's bad producing has brought the rehearsal to a grinding halt. Gilligan reports that Ginger refuses to play the maid. She is back in her hut, crying. Mr. Howell throws a fit: "There's one thing I can't stand . . . temperament," as Jim Backus performs a terrific tantrum himself, stomping on his hat and storming off the stage.

Of course, Mrs. Howell as Cleopatra proves to be terrible, complete with a ridiculously throaty voice that would make a frog croak. The jealous Ginger compares Mrs. Howell's acting to that of Mr. Ed, but the joke is on her, since neither Mrs. nor Mr. Howell have seen the famous televisual horse. Apparently, talking animal shows are not popular among the blue bloods of 1960s America.

As usual, Gilligan plays the peacekeeper. He explains to Mrs. Howell why Ginger needs to play Cleopatra. Mrs. Howell relents, feeling shame for her former selfishness. She kindly pretends to have laryngitis so Ginger can perform. At the actual performance, the conflict between Ginger and Mrs. Howell proves immaterial, since Gilligan has to play all of the other roles. Gilligan ends up playing the maid. He changes quickly and reappears as the royal messenger, and then as a slave. In the coda to the episode, as Mr. Howell dreams of bringing his play to Broadway, the Skipper asks what Gilligan thought about his performance as Mark Antony. While Gilligan will not respond, a parrot he has befriended on the island does: "Terrible!" is the bird's accurate pronouncement on the Skipper's skills as a thespian.

The character behavior in the "Angel on the Island" episode of *Gilligan's Island* serves as a literal enactment of Erving Goffman's thesis in his masterpiece of postwar social psychology, *The Presentation of Self in Everyday Life.* The book's argument is that human beings perform their entire lives, regulating their projection of self as if on a stage. Goffman thus builds a dramaturgical sociology: "The very structure of the self can be seen in terms of how we arrange for such performances in our Anglo-American society" (252).

In the preface to the book, Goffman begins, "The perspective employed in this report is that of the theatrical performance; the principles derived are dramaturgical ones. I shall consider the way in which the individual in ordinary work situations presents himself and his activity to others" (xi). *Gilligan's Island* expresses Goffman's thesis at many levels of experience. First, as a fellow participant in postwar American social life, the show can be seen as data for Goffman's arguments. The castaways function in similar terms to the real people on the Shetland Islands that the sociologist studied during his research for the book. However, as a sitcom, *Gilligan's Island* is not only data but also an active representation. *Gilligan's Island* thus becomes, not data for how people behave observationally, but a representation machine for how people should perform if we want to make the world a better place. While other sitcoms back away from the fascinating central metaphor of television—we are watching people play ourselves and learning from it—via the excuse of performance (it is not unsettlingly artificial that Ricky Ricardo is singing and dancing because he "is" a band leader), *Gilligan's Island* strips away all of this pretense. There is no possible reason these shipwrecked victims should be performing all day, and yet they do so obsessively.

Virtually the first example Goffman provides of performance in everyday life is directly resonant with the representational practices of *Gilligan's Island.* Early in the introduction, Goffman quotes from Willard Waller's article "The Rating and Dating Complex," a postwar sociology article published in the *American Sociological Review.* The study highlights the behavior of college coeds who pretend to be answering phone calls from many prospective dates. It turns out many of these calls are simply meant as performance for the other coeds to be jealous of their popularity. Goffman explains the behavior in general terms: "When an individual appears in the presence of others, there will usually be some reason for him to mobilize his activity so that it will convey an impression to others which is in his interests to convey" (4).

Such behavior forms the material for the plot of an entire *Gilligan's Island* episode, "The Postman Cometh." Once a week, Mary Ann puts a message in a bottle and sends it to her boyfriend, Horace Higgenbotham from Kansas. However, in the teaser to this episode, the radio announcer informs the castaways that Horace has recently become engaged to a socialite. The castaways cowardly elect Gilligan to be the one to break the sad news to Mary Ann. When Gilligan attempts to do so, he is drawn into another layer of performativity. Mary Ann is listening to her favorite soap opera, *Old Doctor Young,* on the radio. The plot is about a man trying to tell a woman about her X-ray results. Gilligan listens intently because it is the same situation that he must confront. However, the drama of the soap opera causes Gilligan to lose his nerve, and he leaves without telling Mary Ann the bad news.

The Professor gallantly agrees to step in and do Gilligan's job. However, he too fails to complete the job when he misreads the reason for Mary Ann's crying. While cooking mushrooms, she is crying at the events on the soap opera, not her own misery. The Professor loses his resolve; he, like Gilligan, fails to tell Mary Ann the truth.

Trying to be helpful, Ginger tells the other castaways that Mary Ann needs a dream man to replace her boyfriend. Mrs. Howell trains Gilligan in romance using Charles Boyer as a model, while Ginger teaches the Professor to be Cary Grant; the Skipper will be a John Wayne cowboy for Mary Ann. Predictably, these performances prove disastrous. Gilligan wears a beret and does a bad French accent. Skipper enters Mary Ann's hut dressed as a marshal, complete with a starfish badge on his chest. The Professor enters doing his hilarious Cary Grant impersonation: "Judy, Judy, Judy."

Mary Ann runs screaming away from these lunatics, thinking the men have truly gone crazy. However, she then overhears them talking. She too misreads the data: she mistakenly believes the men are being so nice to her because she is going to die from having eaten poisonous mushrooms. As act 2 begins, Mary Ann listens again to the soap opera to take her mind off her own worries. The soap opera doctor advises a woman to be truthful with her friends. Mary Ann resolves to apply this lesson to her own situation.

Mary Ann comes to thank Gilligan and the Skipper for helping her. Mr. Howell says it is a small loss. Mary Ann is horrified. When the castaways start planning a party, Mary Ann runs away crying again. Predicting Hollywood films about soap opera obsession, such as *Nurse Betty* (Neil LaBute, 2000), in one of the show's signature dream sequences, Mary Ann wakes up in a hospital bed, within the plot of her favorite radio soap opera. The castaways take on the major roles. Mrs. Howell, the nurse, says she has a fatal disease. Mr. Howell is a doctor, Dr. Zorba Gillespie. Mary Ann demands to see either Old or Young Doctor Young. Mrs. Howell says they are unavailable, preparing a new medical show for television. Instead, the hospital has flown in three experts: Gilligan is Dr. Boyer. Skipper is Old Doc Dillon from the Old West. The Professor says she has Roomus Igloomus, a disease that comes from eating poisonous mushrooms. Ginger plays a nurse too. "Walk this way," says Ginger, setting up the famous wiggle-walk Hollywood joke in which all of the male characters follow her, imitating her sexy locomotion.

Ginger wakes up Mary Ann from her reverie. Gilligan finally tells the truth, that Horace got married. Mary Ann is nonplussed, confessing that Horace was "a real creep" to her. Mary Ann explains that she just wanted the castaways to think she had a boyfriend too, since Ginger is so beautiful. Not only does "The Postman Cometh" predict a range of soap opera/reality Hollywood comedies, such as *Soapdish* (Michael Hoffman, 1991), it is a treasure trove for the importance of performance in everyday life as hypothesized by Goffman. In specific terms, the reveal at the end of the plot is that Mary Ann merely invented a pretense for sending love letters back to Kansas to perform her desirability in competition with Ginger's. But more generally, multiple layers of performance render the castaways' lives on the island as a rich and fertile playground for imaginative experience. They act for one another to impress their rivals, but they also act in the hopes that they will make their fellow human beings feel better.

Building from Simone de Beauvoir's existential feminist analysis, Goffman understands female behavior as performative:

> Confronting man, woman is always play-acting; she lies when she makes believe that she accepts her status as the inessential other, she lies when she presents to him an imaginary personage through mimicry, costume, studied phrases. These histrionics require a constant tension: when with her husband, or with her lover, every woman is more or less conscious of the thought, "I am not being myself." (112–13)

In its stereotypic portrayal of Ginger and Mary Ann as opposite rivals, *Gilligan's Island*'s interest in performativity generally replicates Goffman's sexism. However, the performances in *Gilligan's Island* indicate that something far more complex is being represented, ever-changing roles that result in not just rivalry but deep friendship. This, I believe, is the reason for *Gilligan's Island's* long-standing popularity. The castaways perform our foibles, but also how to overcome them to be timeless friends.

Consider the complex representation of performance in the episode "The Second Ginger Grant." As the episode begins, Ginger, parodying Jayne Mansfield parodying Marilyn Monroe, performs "I Wanna Be Loved by You" on the bamboo stage. The castaways, and Mary Ann in particular, rave about how wonderful Ginger is: "I'd give anything to be like Ginger Grant, a real movie star." Mary Ann backs up, trips over a rock, and gets knocked unconscious. When Gilligan revives Mary Ann, she insists (in Ginger's voice) that she is indeed Ginger, not Mary Ann.

The Professor can find no physical cause of Mary Ann's illness. He instead explains the psychology of the situation. The Professor prescribes performance as the cure, to go along with Mary Ann's fantasy. "One of us will have to be Mary Ann," he deduces, assigning Ginger to the role. Thus, in this episode, Ginger has to play herself, in Mary Ann's body, and Mary Ann, in her own body, not to mention the fact that Tina Louise and Dawn Wells are already performing these roles as fictional characters.

Back in their hut, Mr. Howell tries to explain the confusing situation to Mrs. Howell as they try to find a wig for Ginger to play Mary Ann. After much explanation, Mrs. Howell still does not understand. Frustrated, Mr. Howell gasps, using a dramaturgical Goffman metaphor: "It's getting so that you can't tell the players without a program."

For act 2, the castaways must perform as if Mary Ann is Ginger, and vice versa. Mary Ann wears a leopard-skin two-piece suit, sexy attire that in any other episode Mary Ann would never think of wearing. Researching a play, Mary Ann coaxes

Gilligan to play her boyfriend, Scott, in the scene. Gilligan reads his lines incompetently, but Mary Ann paws Gilligan lasciviously during the entire scene. When she finally kisses him passionately, Gilligan runs away screaming.

A scene of performative levity interrupts the plot. As the men put the finishing touches on resizing Ginger's clothes so that Mary Ann can wear them, the three men also do imitations of Mary Ann-as-Ginger's walk. Ginger laughs, asking the men to redo the walking because it is so funny. Mrs. Howell comes in and joins in with the laughs as well. For her part, Ginger does a terrible job filling in for Mary Ann. Ginger as Mary Ann has made fish pie for dinner. However, it is inedible. It is just a whole fish covered in dough, uncooked.

The turning point of the episode occurs when Ginger forgets to wear her Mary Ann wig while doing the laundry. When Mary Ann sees her, she collapses from the trauma. The Professor examines Mary Ann, but she has fallen into a catatonic state. The Professor tries using hypnosis to cure Mary Ann. The Professor snaps his fingers, and Mary Ann awakens out of the coma. She is upset that she saw herself, Ginger, at the laundry. The Professor explains that it was just a trick of the island light. He rehypnotizes Mary Ann. Gilligan stands at the window. He gets hypnotized, too, by mistake. The Professor's instructions are, "When I hear the name Mary Ann, I will become Mary Ann." The Professor wakes up Mary Ann and tries his trick. However, it fails; Mary Ann continues to insist she is Ginger.

The cure works instead on Gilligan. The boy in his bathtub now insists he is Mary Ann. The Professor quickly cures Gilligan, but the problem of Mary Ann continues to perplex the castaways. The Professor has another idea, in fact, the central idea of *Gilligan's Island*. To cure the problem, they will ask Mary Ann to put on a show. They know that Mary Ann will not be able to perform as Ginger, and this realization will cause Mary Ann to return to normal.

At the show, Mr. Howell plays Ed Sullivan, serving as the emcee. Mary Ann sings "I Wanna Be Loved by You" horribly off-key. She forgets the words. She asks for Mr. Howell to start the record again. She trips over her boa, falls off the stage, and passes out again. Mary Ann is back to normal. The episode's coda is devoted to the friendship between Ginger and Mary Ann. Ginger is wearing a miniskirt because all the alterations to Ginger's clothes for Mary Ann left little material to work with. Unlike Goffman's hypothesis that women's performances are devoted exclusively to competition with other women, *Gilligan's Island* builds a community of friends. None of the men ever compete for romantic relationships with either Mary Ann or Ginger. When Mary Ann suffers, Ginger comes to her aid. As an entertainer, Sherwood Schwartz believes that entertainment is the cure for what ails us. In "The Second Ginger Grant," the help that Mary Ann needs is the loving performance of her friends. Putting on a show, both literally and symbolically, is the response *Gilligan's Island* proposes to our significant troubles, an apt response from Schwartz, who abandoned the study of biology in order to devote his life to making people laugh.

Not just limited to gender relations, performance is the fundamental building block of the community in *Gilligan's Island.* Stranded on the island with almost no other resources, playacting is virtually the only tool that the castaways have to solve their problems. Goffman argues that while America is a class-stratified society, all social classes perform their identities. This radically democratic vision of social life is fully endorsed by *Gilligan's Island.* Like Melville in *Moby-Dick,* Schwartz offers the island as a social microcosm of the nation, where all social classes, the laborers like the Skipper and Mary Ann and the wealthy Howells, mix.

In his exploration of performance in the workspace, Goffman argues that people must perform at work as if they are always busy. That is the very definition of work, he assumes.

81

"Make-work, along with other aspects of decorum in workplaces, is usually seen as the particular burden of those of low estate. . . . It should be plain that while persons who are obliged to make-work and make-no-work are likely to be on the opposite sides of the track, they must yet adapt themselves to the same side of the footlights" (110–11). Thus, Goffman argues that bosses and workers, while the content of their performance is quite different, must both perform—that is, construct their identity out of an act that will be interpreted by the others around them, their audience: "Individuals with wildly different social roles live in the same climate of dramaturgical experience. The talks that comedians and scholars give are quite different, but their talk about their talk is quite similar" (176). This is one of the more profound lessons of *Gilligan's Island.* No matter what the crisis, the putting on of a show—either on the stage or off of it—is the solution.

The Howells, of course, are the central characters around which Schwartz builds his performative presentation of American social class. In many episodes, the Howells must readjust their performance when they believe their fortune to have collapsed in their absence from the mainland. As but one example, "Agonized Labor" (season 2, episode 44, November 11, 1965) begins when Gilligan and the Skipper hear on the radio that Howell Industries has gone bankrupt. Immediately, the castaways enter performance mode. The Skipper helps Gilligan practice how to tell Mr. Howell that he is bankrupt. After much delaying, Gilligan finally tells the Howells that they are broke. However, each of the castaways' attempts to help Mr. Howell's destroyed ego is met with disaster. A bee in the flowers Mary Ann brings attacks Mr. Howell. The Professor fixes Mr. Howell's practice polo pony, but as soon as Mr. Howell climbs up on it, it collapses. Act 2 begins as the castaways learn the stakes of their act 1 failure: Mrs. Howell reads a suicide note from Mr. Howell.

The castaways again jump into action, breaking up into three search parties, chasing after Mr. Howell, who stumbles through the jungle to find an apt place to kill himself. Ginger begins the proceedings by relating the day's events to a movie she was in with Rock Hudson. He was the richest man in the world, who walked to a high mountain and jumped off when he lost all his money.

For his part, Mr. Howell knows little more than the movies as he tries to find the correct performative metaphor now that his wealth has abandoned him. He wants to wade into the ocean like James Mason in *A Star Is Born* (George Cukor, 1954). They find Mr. Howell and bring him back to the huts before he can hurt himself. When Gilligan says Mr. Howell will have to work for his living now, the former millionaire wants to go back to the ocean to enact his suicide plan.

The Professor has an idea, again resorting to performance. They will teach the Howells how to work. Each of the castaways takes turns training the Howells in a trade. The Skipper teaches seamanship to Mr. Howell. Mary Ann teaches sewing to Mrs. Howell. Ginger teaches method acting to Mrs. Howell, ensuring that she can die melodramatically.

That night, the Howells get to perform their new skills, as domestic servants. Mr. Howell is the waiter and Mrs. Howell is the cook. At first, things seem to go well with their new performative roles: they set a beautiful table. However, Mr. Howell spills the soup all over the castaways' laps. Mrs. Howell explodes the coconuts by cooking them whole. Luckily, the failed performative roles are short lived. The radio reports that the Howell financial structure is intact. It was the *Powell* fortune that was ruined!

Beyond work roles, as in the plays of Shakespeare, much of the performing in *Gilligan's Island* revolves around love and relationships. In "The Matchmaker" (season 1, episode 25, March 20, 1965), Mrs. Howell laments missing the opening of the opera season. Bored, she looks out her window to discover Gilligan helping Mary Ann. The dowager decides to arrange

Gilligan's wedding to Mary Ann so that she can have a society season: she sees the youngsters as Romeo and Juliet.

Mrs. Howell insists to her husband that they demonstrate their perfect marriage to Gilligan and Mary Ann, to serve as role models. They invite Gilligan to a romantic dinner with Mary Ann at the Howells' hut. Mary Ann arrives in a dress. Gilligan is in his familiar red shirt, but buttoned up. Mr. and Mrs. Howell depart, blowing out the candles. Gilligan and Mary Ann awkwardly sit in the mood lighting.

The Howells listen in, bringing in champagne, trying to rescue the disastrous date. It is the twentieth anniversary of *their* proposal dinner. However, Mr. and Mrs. Howell argue over the details of that night (what they ate, what street in New York City the restaurant was on, the color of her dress). Gilligan tries to drink to twenty years of wedded bliss, but Mr. and Mrs. Howell are in the midst of a fight in which they name all of the things about each other that annoy them. Mrs. Howell says she will never speak to Mr. Howell again.

As act 2 begins, the castaways now must act to save the Howells' marriage. Mr. Howell moves into the men's hut, while Mrs. Howell moves into the women's. The castaways devise their own romantic dinner to repair the marriage. The Skipper and Ginger play Mr. and Mrs. Howell as they rehearse the dinner, again demonstrating that every relationship on the island is fair game for reenactment by any of the other castaways in an endless permutation of combinations. The night of the dinner, Mr. Howell bemoans, "These playacting shenanigans." Ginger does a hula dance from her most memorable film, *The Hula Girl and the Fullback*. Despite Gilligan's antics—he spills soup over the married couple—Mr. and Mrs. Howell finally reconcile, thanks to the performative efforts of the castaways.

The apotheosis of performance in *Gilligan's Island* is the episode "Not Guilty" in which the castaways literally must perform to save their community. As the episode begins, Gilligan fishes in a crate containing coconuts wrapped in newspaper. One of the old papers has an article declaring that one of the passengers aboard the *Minnow* killed a man, Randolph Blake, in Hawaii the night before the storm that shipwrecked the boat. A cinephile, Gilligan immediately declares that the butler did it. The Skipper explains that they do not have a butler. Gilligan decides to look for the most innocent looking castaway. His suspicions seem confirmed when he visits the Professor, horrified to discover that the scientist has just perfected his bamboo guillotine. "It's going to eliminate a lot of manpower," declares the Professor, which Gilligan interprets ominously, despite the Professor's intention of using the device to cut open coconuts.

Gilligan convinces the Skipper of the Professor's guilt. They run to warn the girls of the danger, only to discover Mary Ann and Ginger cooking poison made of wild oleanders. While they want to get rid of the mice infesting their hut, the men misinterpret their comment, "And if it works, we're going to try to get rid of some other horrible creatures around here, too."

As the first act comes to a close, Gilligan and the Skipper begin to suspect each other, delivering the narrative's theme about how paranoia destroys community. Finally, the castaways decide to put aside their suspicions and work as a group to solve the mystery. The castaways talk through the events of the night before they left on their journey aboard the *Minnow*. The Professor confesses that he knew Blake. They argued that night because Blake tried to take credit for a scientific paper the Professor had written. In a bout of sitcom coincidence, all of the castaways quarreled with Blake the night before the cruise. Blake worked for the Howells, Ginger had a date with him, and Mary Ann knew him because they were from the same hometown.

As is now predictable, the castaways decide on a performative method to resolve their crisis. Gilligan explains that they must reenact the crime, as happens on *Perry Mason* (CBS, 1957–66). The Skipper gets his spear gun, as the newspaper article reports that this was the murder weapon. Gilligan takes the role of Randolph Blake. In turn, each of the castaways confronts Blake as they did the night of the murder. As the last of them, Ginger, runs out of the room shouting, "I hate you," Gilligan slams the door, triggering the firing of the spear gun. The Skipper concludes that the death of Blake must have been an accident.

In the episode's coda, the radio reports the exact findings that the castaways discovered through their performances. The slamming of a door triggered the accidental firing of the spear gun, thus clearing all the castaways of murder charges. Gilligan is so happy that their performance worked out the solution just like the police did, he causes the spear gun to fire again, severing the rope holding up the Skipper's hammock, causing the boat captain to comically flop onto the floor.

Gilligan, the Natural Man

Performance and natural history studies converge in an analysis of the episode "Beauty Is as Beauty Does" (season 2, episode 38, September 23, 1965) in which Gilligan's forward thinking derails a misguided beauty contest between the island's three women, Ginger, Mary Ann, and Mrs. Howell. The episode begins with the Skipper, Mr. Howell, and the Professor arguing over who is the most beautiful woman on the island. They decide to hold a beauty contest, with Gilligan as the judge. In the meantime, Gilligan befriends Gladys the ape, despite her annoying antics: she wears his hat, and she steals his banana just as he is about to eat it. However, as the human tensions increase, with each male castaway lobbying for his favorite female, Gilligan finds a much-needed confidant in Gladys. Gilligan laments to her, "The friendly little beauty contest [has turned out to be] as friendly as World War II." At the end of the episode, Gilligan decides on the winner of the Miss Castaway

Contest: Gladys, because, as Gilligan explains, she is the only one born on the island.

In their defense of *The Andy Griffith Show* (CBS, 1960–68) for *The Sitcom Reader,* John O'Leary and Rick Worland argue that

> the "Idiot Sitcom" era, which Brooks and Marsh date from the early to late 1950s . . . featured gimmicks to drive the comedy in which the characters are cartoonish and plots are "restricted to farce" (Marc, *Demographic Vistas,* 56). Shows such as . . . *Gilligan's Island* . . . would seem to affirm Brooks and Marsh's derisive designation. Rather than being built on gimmicks, however, *The Andy Griffith Show* harkens back to the affectionate and incisive rural humor identified with Mark Twain and Will Rogers. (76)

Conversely, I argue that it is precisely *Gilligan's Island*'s retreat into the abstract natural primitive—Gilligan is an American Adam, to return to R. W. B. Lewis's foundational American studies formulation—that allows the show to indict nostalgic formulations of the American rural.

Gilligan's Island serves as a most unexpected solution to C. P. Snow's problem of the two cultures (science and the humanities): it is a show that engages key questions about the scientific relationship between humans and animals and does so with aesthetic and narrative virtuosity. Jane R. Goodall's book *Performance and Evolution in the Age of Darwin: Out of the Natural Order* (2002) resonates closely with the representation of the natural world in *Gilligan's Island.* Profoundly transcending Snow's two cultures, Goodall argues that nineteenth-century ideas of human evolution found complementary expression in Darwinian science and P. T. Barnum's theatrical performance. Early in the book, Goodall studies the appearance of apes and humans on the stage together in the nineteenth century. Goodall's most compelling textual analysis concerns the 1825 French pantomime play, *Jocko; or, The Brazilian Ape.* Goodall argues:

> Two hands reach for each other, their index fingers almost touching but not quite, so that the space between them recalls for a moment the gap between the outstretched fingers of God and Adam on the ceiling of the Sistine Chapel. . . . The hands are those of a child and a monkey, two dancing figures depicted in their parallel roles in the sentimental drama. . . . Their *pas de deux* is choreographed as a sequence of mirror images: the child prays and the ape copies the attitude; the ape jumps around and the child does likewise. . . . Through this symmetrical and sentimental plot, Jocko emphasizes a fundamental equivalence between ape and human. . . . Jocko has replaced Adam as the missing link, which is no longer located in the metaphysical space between the divine and animal kingdoms, and is now situated in the natural world, between animal and man. (50)

Goodall argues that the Darwinian revolution did not come to the nineteenth century as a shock but instead as a gradual gathering of scientific understandings that dovetailed with contemporary theatrical performances. Similarly, in the technologically tumultuous 1960s, *Gilligan's Island* constructs Gilligan as the American Adam via his relationship with apes. In six different episodes, Gilligan befriends an ape while all the other castaways abhor such close contact with nature. In episode 19, "Gilligan Meets Jungle Boy" (season 1, February 6, 1965), while Gilligan is peeling a banana, he thinks he hears a gorilla scream, but it is in reality a jungle boy. The boy playfully swings on a vine; Gilligan tries it, but he does not have the requisite dexterity to move around the jungle this way, thus replicating Jocko's pas de deux a century earlier.

The Skipper crosses the species barrier in "Beauty Is as Beauty Does" (September 23, 1965).

But most strikingly, the nexus between performance, humanity, and the animal world is engaged by the beauty contest episode. Goodall's Michelangelo analysis serves as a critical template for understanding the *Gilligan's Island* imagery. Early in the episode, Gilligan retreats to the forest to avoid the corrupt manipulations of the men, who are trying to solicit his vote. With no one else to talk to, Gilligan confides in his chimpanzee friend, Gladys. In a direct replication of the Jocko pantomime, Gilligan holds her hand and talks with her in a tree. When the Skipper arrives to influence his vote, Gilligan interrupts the corruption by restaging Michelangelo's painting, coaxing the Skipper to shake hands with Gladys, which he very nearly does until he realizes Gilligan's folly.

At the end of her book, Goodall reflects on fin-de-siècle ballet as it was performed on the nineteenth-century stage as an indication of the contradictions of gender implicit in Darwinism. On the one hand, science had turned cultural attention to the anatomical facts of all bodies, male and female. In a bizarre reversal of modern ballet's insistence on anorectics, nineteenth-century critic Gautier praised Mademoiselle Essler's dancing for her body's portly hiding of what he considered to be the hideous bone structure of thin women: "Her bosom is full, a rare thing in the world of entrechats where the twin hills and the snowy mountains of which students and minor poets sing appear totally unknown. Nor can one see moving on her back those two bony triangles which are like the roots of torn off wings" (192). On the other hand, the ballet reveled in the abstract beauty of the ballerina in seemingly effortless flight. Goodall cites Albert Smith's 1847 satire, *The Natural History of the Ballet Girl*: "Smith recount[s] the fantasy of the ballet girl as a magical species who transcends physical life, having been initiated as a child into the realms of the fairies where she once danced by moonlight on the primrose banks" (190). The nineteenth-century fusion of evolutionary science and ballet haunts Ginger's beauty contest performance.

Ginger emerges onto the stage as a bodily imitation of Marilyn Monroe, seeping modern sexuality, with no pretence to emulate the ballerina fairies of the nineteenth century. However, Gilligan cringes every time he takes notice of her corporeal body. Similarly, the Professor and Mr. Howell attack Ginger's body with their blow guns, bringing the violent competition from the Western mainland continuous from Stephano and Trinculo in *The Tempest* to the American military in 1960s Vietnam. In response to this, Gilligan cannot help but return the island to an earlier natural state in which Gladys is the deserving winner precisely because she is neither human nor American.

"Beauty Is as Beauty Does" ends with a meditation on human versus animal intelligence: As the castaways spy Gilligan's notes taken during the contest, they discover that he was playing tic-tac-toe the whole time. Gilligan explains, "I didn't want you to see that I lost every game!" In this and other episodes, *Gilligan's Island* adopts a revealing attitude toward human beings, one in which the other castaways deviate from the naturalness of Gilligan, who remains in closer contact with the animal world, a stance that the show validates. As Goodall's study attests, this represents a significant departure from the social Darwinist nature of the nineteenth-century theatrical tradition on which *Gilligan's Island*—especially given its slapstick and vaudeville comedy trappings—otherwise depends.

These various analyses of performativity in *Gilligan's Island* highlight the important place of the show in continuity with the history of the sitcom. *Gilligan's Island's* interest in performativity describes the entire history of the sitcom, from *I Love Lucy* to *The Dick Van Dyke Show* to *Seinfeld*. While these other shows build performance into their given circumstances, *Gilligan's Island* does not, instead most radically suggesting—as Goffman's research confirmed—that regular people like us, not just television celebrities, also "perform" as a basic function of our existence.

The Afterlife
of *Gilligan's Island*

After cancellation, *Gilligan's Island* found great success in the United States as a morning and afternoon UHF staple in syndication. The most successfully syndicated sitcom on the global television market, *Gilligan's Island,* because of its easily understood stock characters and its catchy theme song, became a ubiquitously understood cultural reference. The ill-fated narrative closure of the made-for-TV movie sequels to the original episodes (1978's top-rated *Rescue from Gilligan's Island*; 1979's *The Castaways on Gilligan's Island*; and the much maligned disaster, 1981's *The Harlem Globetrotters on Gilligan's Island*) did not dampen fans' love of the original ninety-eight episodes.

The legacy of *Gilligan's Island* on American television is profound. One cannot help but see the game show *Survivor* as merely a depressing devolution of *Gilligan's Island,* as contestants plot to cheat one another to win money by surviving on a desert island. Compared to the game show's Machiavellian dynamics, the humanism of Sherwood Schwartz's 1960s vision of island utopia seems as much needed in 2012 as it was in 1965.

Jason Mittell's hope that J. J. Abrams's ABC drama would not become a true disaster like *Gilligan's Island* notwithstanding, the triumph of *Lost* lies in its direct continuities with *Gilligan's Island.* In each show, the not-so-hidden subtext is that, despite both sets of castaways' stated desire to escape from the island as quickly as possible, the island of exile proves to be a utopian place in which to begin anew the project of communitarian human civilization. Yet not all contemporary films and television shows share the utopian communitarian impulse of *Gilligan's Island.* In *Cast Away* (Robert Zemeckis, 2000), FedEx executive Chuck Noland crash-lands on an isolated island. He is marooned alone for years, having only his volleyball, Wilson, with whom to converse. Unlike *Gilligan's Island, Cast Away* devotes the second half of its narrative to Chuck learning to readjust to life back on the mainland after he is rescued. While the television movie sequels to *Gilligan's Island* played with the idea of rescue, they quickly reverted to the castaways back on their idyllic island, because on the island was the lure of community. *Lost,* too, equivocates in this way, having some of the castaways, the "Oceanic 6," return to civilization (only to work desperately, like their *Gilligan's Island* counterparts, to return to the island). However, like Gilligan, who insists that the community on the island is the best life they could hope for, *Lost* foregrounds its believers in the island's utopian possibilities.

While John Locke (Terry O'Quinn) is *Lost's* most flamboyant island utopian, the example of Rose (L. Scott Caldwell) most directly links back to the tradition of *Gilligan's Island.* We meet Rose in the pilot episode. A quiet African American woman,

Rose, we come to learn, never gives up hope that her husband, a "tailie" (someone seated in the tail section of the plane), is still alive. Midway through the second season, Rose and her husband, Bernard (Sam Nadler), are reunited. The tailies had in fact landed on the other side of the island, which we learn in the episode "The Other 48 Days" (season 2, episode 32, November 16, 2005). In the late season 2 episode "S.O.S." (episode 43, April 12, 2006), Bernard stubbornly attempts to build a large SOS sign on the beach out of rocks, even though no one will help him. At the end of the episode, in one of *Lost's* signature emotionally startling moments, Rose and Bernard argue over the sign. Rose refuses to help him with the sign; Bernard accuses her of giving up. We come to learn Rose's secret: she had been suffering a terminal illness back in Los Angeles and was going to Australia for a charlatan's cure as a last desperate attempt to stay alive. However, on the island, Rose is no longer ill; the island has cured her. Rose and Bernard share a tender moment where they vow never to leave the island as the episode ends.

Abrams's commitment to castaways who would rather stay lost than return to the corrupt mainland is its central inheritance from *Gilligan's Island*. In episode after episode of Schwartz's show, comic equivalents of *Lost's* Bernard and Rose sequence are enacted. In "Ghost a Go-Go" (season 2, episode 63, March 24, 1966), Gilligan gives the clearest defense of refusing rescue in the entire series: "I don't want to leave. . . . I had fun here," he explains as the castaways prepare to follow the instructions of a "ghost" (in reality, a criminal in a white sheet) to use his boat to leave the island. Luckily, the Professor's rationalist suspicions dovetail with Gilligan's desire to remain on the island. The castaways make dummies of themselves to put into the boat to test the ghost's intentions. The ghost proceeds to blow up the boat as soon as the dummy castaways are safely aboard.

The core narrative of *Gilligan's Island* is about Gilligan doing something dumb such that the castaways do not get rescued.

In "Gilligan Goes Gung-Ho," the castaways never have time to light an SOS sign made of wood and flammable material, since Sherriff Gilligan has locked all of the castaways, including himself, into a jail built into a cave. In "Splashdown" (season 3, episode 90, February 20, 1967), the castaways hear on the radio that a NASA space mission will be flying directly over the island. The castaways build an SOS sign out of logs and light it with Mr. Howell's brandy. However, Gilligan accidentally catches his pants leg on fire, and in the subsequent chaos, he knocks the signal logs into disarray. The astronauts look down at the Pacific Ocean, and spot the island and the fire burning on it. However, the sign now spells out SOL; as one of the astronaut's name is Sol, NASA believes the sign merely to be a patriotic tribute to the mission. The Skipper makes Gilligan spell SOS on a chalkboard hundreds of times as punishment, but he already knows the lesson that Rose teaches Bernard with love: to stay on the island is to find a love uncorrupted by the diseases, both physical and spiritual, of the mainland.

The subtext of *Gilligan's Island* is that the castaways' stated desire to escape from exile on the island is distinctly misguided. Only Gilligan, the American Adam, is intuitively smart enough to realize that the island is a far better place to live than the corrupt American mainland. What Rose comes to learn from her island, Gilligan knew almost immediately in the middle of the 1960s. What is remarkable about this from a television studies perspective is that it turns out that so-called quality television, which is purported to have rebelled against the inanity of popular commercial television shows such as *Gilligan's Island,* is in fact far more interconnected than we have been led to believe. For example, *Northern Exposure* (CBS, 1990–95), Joshua Brand and John Falsey's charming sequel to *St. Elsewhere* (NBC, 1982–88), is a show that mimics the comedy of *Gilligan's Island.* While *Gilligan's Island* is set in the tropical Pacific and *Northern Exposure* in frigid Alaska, both shows propose that their communities are superior to the corrupt American mainland.

The ill-fated SOS sign in "Splashdown" (February 20, 1967).

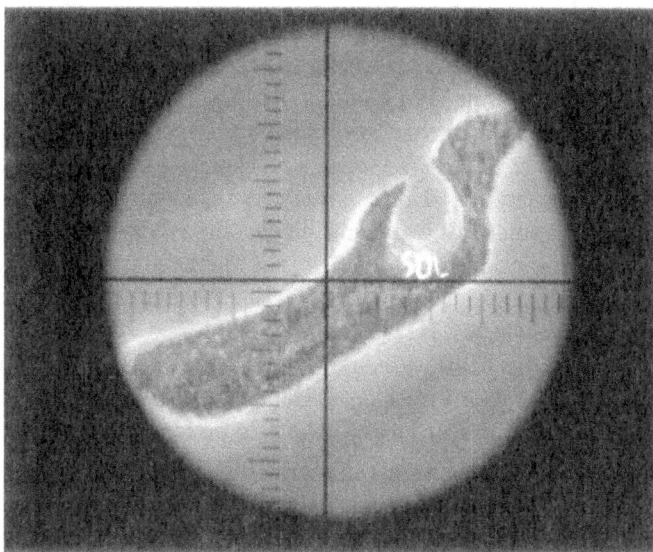

Gilligan misspells SOS in "Splashdown" (February 20, 1967).

Rose and Bernard's aborted sign in the "S.O.S." episode of *Lost* (April 12, 2006).

A "fish out of water" sitcom housed in an hour-long dramedy, *Northern Exposure* features Dr. Joel Fleischman (Rob Morrow), a New York doctor condemned to pay off his medical loans in the isolated backwoods town of Cicely, Alaska. There, he discovers a microcosm of social misfits. In an astonishing sequence, Ruth-Anne (Peg Phillips), the proprietor of the town's small grocery, laments the visit of her son from Atlanta. Speaking as if the son is a serial killer, Ruth finally admits that what she is ashamed of is that he is a stockbroker. In both *Gilligan's Island*, a popular vast wasteland sitcom, and *Northern Exposure,* a quality television 1990s dramedy, the mainland is corrupt and can be fought against only from the utopian peripheries of the last American states, Hawaii and Alaska.

I began this book with a reflection on the focused plot concentrations of Samuel Beckett's *Waiting for Godot* and *Gilligan's Island,* the notion that great drama is to be found in sticking a small number of characters in a symbolic box to express basic tenets of human behavior. Since the cancellation of *Gilligan's Island,* if not inspired by the comic styling of Sherwood Schwartz, certainly indebted to his legacy, American popular culture has continued to mine the existential experiments of Samuel Beckett. In *The Unofficial* Gilligan's Island *Handbook,* Joey Green reports, "In the fall of 1982, members of the Harvard Lampoon, dressed in black and seated on stools, performed an episode of *Gilligan's Island* ('Seer Gilligan') as an existential play in beatnik [inflection] for one week at Harvard's Experimental Theatre" (15). In the "Seer Gilligan" episode (season 2, episode 55, January 27, 1966), the teaser sequence reveals that Gilligan can suddenly read the other castaways' minds. At first, the Professor does not believe in this supernatural power, stating unequivocally that clairvoyance "is a scientific impossibility." However, when Gilligan reads the Professor's mind in order to state the atomic weight of aluminum, the Professor is dumbfounded.

After some comic hilarity as the castaways try to discover how Gilligan reads minds—Mr. Howell suspects it must be something he eats, which causes him to get sick trying to consume all that Gilligan does—the Professor figures out that sunflower seeds used by ancient islanders for clairvoyance are the culprit. Gilligan shares a huge bag of seeds with the castaways, who eat them ravenously. The castaways scheme the entire night to get Gilligan to reveal the location of the plant that produces the seeds. The next day, fights break out all over the island as the castaways read one another's minds. For example, the Skipper leaves Gilligan in a huff after he finds out that his little buddy was thinking how fat he is.

The Professor remarks that these are the first real fights they have had since being shipwrecked. The Professor is devastated, since it was his belief that the seeds could have been used to resolve political misunderstandings and bring about world peace. The Professor leaves equally angry after he finds out that Gilligan thinks his idea for world peace is stupid. After he can no longer stand the castaways fighting with one another, Gilligan burns the bush. The Professor congratulates Gilligan for being the only one smart enough to destroy the ancient seed-producing bush.

While it is impossible for me to know the details of the Harvard production of "Seer Gilligan," the idea to perform the episode as an existential play certainly intensifies some of the dramatic minimalism of the show. The legacy of *Gilligan's Island*'s minimalism can be tracked intertextually. In the Irish film version of Samuel Beckett's *Act without Words I,* a resonance can be identified with Schwartz's show. Beckett's mime play was written in 1956 and concerns a man on an empty stage who is terrorized by a stagehand who keeps lowering objects toward the hapless man, only to yank them away when the man comes within reach of them. In 2000, the Irish Film Board commissioned filmmakers to commit performances of all nineteen of Beckett's plays to the screen. Karel Reisz was chosen to shoot the one-act *Act without Words I.* Famous for the British kitchen sink realist film *Saturday Night and Sunday Morning* (1960) and the art house hit *The French Lieutenant's Woman* (1981), Reisz sets *Act without Words I* in a desert, with the unseen stagehand lowering a bottle of water and a banana down to the victim (played by Sean Foley). Every time the man tries to leave the desert, he appears to hit an invisible plastic wall that bounces him back into the camera frame.

Beckett's purpose is to express theatrically the existentialism of Albert Camus in his essay "The Myth of Sisyphus." In that essay, Camus argues that we are wrong to focus on the gods' power over Sisyphus as they condemn him to push the rock up the hill yet again. Instead, Camus emphasizes the triumph of the human spirit as Sisyphus decides to push the rock back up the hill again. Similarly, the victim in *Act without Words I* tries all sorts of schemes to defeat the stagehand. When the water bottle is too high to reach, he piles boxes to climb, at which point the stagehand merely raises the bottle even higher. While the man loses each time, he continues his quest to overcome these horrific circumstances.

Given the minimalism of *Gilligan's Island,* this 1960s sitcom is not all that far afield from Karel Reisz's imagery. Set in a desert with only one character, the play is about finding humanity in a desperate situation of ghastly repetition. The repetitive inanity of *Gilligan's Island*, at the show's best, captures the comedic aspects of the existential condition that so fascinated Camus and Beckett. For example, "Not Guilty" begins with Gilligan and the Skipper excited that they have fished in a crate from the ocean marked food. They are excited to eat something besides coconuts, imagining that the box contains steak or vegetables. Instead, the box contains coconuts! As the stagehand presses on the victim in *Act without Words I* in order to create tragicomedy, existential circumstance from which the core of all human drama is generated, so too does Schwartz press absurdity on his islanders in order to create a more populist form of comedy.

The comparison between the high culture *Act without Words I* and the popular culture *Gilligan's Island* provides a chance to reflect on the fusion of these traditions in recent American film culture. In *Pirates of the Caribbean III: At World's End* (Gore Verbinski, 2007), an astonishing sequence recalls the existential nature of *Gilligan's Island*. Having died at sea, Captain Jack Sparrow (Johnny Depp) wakes up in purgatory. Director Gore Verbinski—an experimental filmmaker who expresses himself in popular Hollywood cinema (the very plot of *The Ring* [Gore Verbinski, 2002] is built around the fact that to watch his experimental film captured on a videotape is to kill its spectator)—films Jack's experience in purgatory as if it were an existential episode of *Gilligan's Island*.

In an otherwise out-of-control Hollywood extravaganza, this seven-minute section of *Pirates of the Caribbean III* is as deftly constructed, both narratively and aesthetically, as one of the dream sequences on *Gilligan's Island*. The sequence begins on a white soundstage, in close-up of Captain Jack sniffing a peanut. As if Charlie Chaplin in *The Gold Rush* (1925), he meticulously prepares himself to consume the morsel, pinning a napkin to his chest. Emulating Errol Flynn as a daring swashbuckler, Jack declares, "Gentlemen, I wash my hands of this weirdness," swinging on a rope to land on the desiccated sand of a tropical island in the middle of which is his stranded ship, the *Black Pearl*. Surrounded by nothing but sand, Jack comes across one isolated stone. He picks up the rock and casts it away. Returning to the base of the ship, he reencounters the rock, far from where it came to rest after he threw it. He reexamines the stone, licks it, and then casts it away yet again. The rock suddenly comes alive as a crab.

Mumbling, "Now we're being followed by rocks, never had that before," he comes across an isolated rope hanging from the ship. This is a virtually identical shot to that in Reisz's *Act without Words I* in which the stagehand lowers a rope to tempt the hapless victim. Captain Jack grabs the rope, only to have it fall unmoored onto the desert floor. The crab summons his friends, who get under the ship and begin moving it. The fallen Captain Jack awakens to witness his ship moving through the desert island, carried by thousands of crabs. Left alone in the image, Jack runs after the boat. As his undead crewmen arrive on the island, the experimental sequence of existential theater comes to a close and the film resumes its status as Hollywood action film blockbuster.

This remarkable experimental scene in a Hollywood blockbuster resonates with the silliness of *Gilligan's Island*. In particular, the episode "Court-Martial" strikes me as a test version of *Pirates of the Caribbean*. Listening to the radio, the Skipper learns that a maritime board of inquiry has fixed the blame for the *Minnow* disaster on the Skipper, calling the captain "completely incompetent." Deciding to hang himself with vines rather than suffer the guilt over dooming his friends, the Skipper leaves for the other side of the island to isolate himself. All the other castaways come to save the Skipper. The Professor builds an intricate apparatus to reenact the night of the storm. During the performance, Gilligan realizes the shipwreck was his fault: he neglected to tie the anchor to the *Minnow* before throwing it overboard. After the commercial, in act 2 of the episode, this time it is Gilligan trying to hang himself. The Skipper and Gilligan decide to go to the other side of the island together, to live out their days there in isolation from the others.

Sleepy, Gilligan asks the Skipper what it would have been like to live in pirate days. Thus initiates the last dream sequence in the series, which mimics an Errol Flynn movie and predicts the world of Captain Jack Sparrow. Admiral Gilligan is the youngest in the fleet, protecting Mrs. Howell, the Queen Mother. The Skipper, the Professor, and Mr. Howell attack the ship as pirates Captain Kidd, Captain Hook, and Long John Silver. Gilligan fights gallantly, but his sword breaks in two, and the pirates force him to walk the plank. At that, the Skipper wakes up Gilligan. They learn from a new report on the radio that new testimony—that there was no mention of the approaching storm on the weather report—exonerates both Gilligan and the Skipper of blame for the shipwrecking of the *Minnow*.

Conclusion: Television in the Age of the DVD

When I began writing about *Bewitched* in 1996, both that magicom and *Gilligan's Island* were airing on local stations as well as basic cable's TV Land many times per day. As I finished drafting this manuscript in 2010, *Gilligan's Island* had long since gone off the air altogether. I am struck by a frightening irony of writing about these formerly ubiquitous sitcoms in an age when their presence on television is dwindling because all the episodes are packaged on DVDs and are available on Netflix and for on-demand downloading. And yet, by what mechanism would a new generation of viewers be drawn to *Gilligan's Island*, which had heretofore run continuously in syndication since the late 1960s? As I prepared to write this manuscript, my children and

I watched all of the episodes of *Gilligan's Island* in the span of just a few weeks. My children thus see *Gilligan's Island* as a very long movie, not the daily ritual that spanned the entirety of my childhood. It is odd that television studies now has the infrastructure to turn to detailed analysis of these shows at precisely the moment that their importance as television fixtures is suddenly disappearing.

Just a few years ago, I could go into my freshman-level "Theater and Mass Media" course and know that when I led with my analysis of Shakespeare's *Hamlet* and "The Producer" episode of *Gilligan's Island,* I could win the hesitant audience over with my hipness. Now, when I ask a roomful of college students if they have ever seen a single episode of *Gilligan's Island,* only a small number of hands go up. My kids' reaction to the show—they love rewatching episodes just as much as I did when I was their age—is encouraging, but they are not a helpful sample for performing sociological analysis. That their father is a television scholar means that they have access to the show in a way that used to be provided merely by turning on a TV set. At what point will people simply stop looking for DVDs of *Gilligan's Island* because it is an ancient show that only old people think is funny? I suppose this is always the crisis of scholarship, that one's once current and beloved objects of study will by necessity go out of date. However, the crisis in television studies, connected as it is to the technologies of the delivery of the medium, seem particularly pertinent and melancholia inducing. The celebration of community in *Gilligan's Island* seems to have been supported, in terms of my reading at any rate, by the delivery of the show *on television.* The show perhaps was able to use inanity as a narrative motivation precisely because, with only three choices, a large majority of viewers were likely to stick with the show.

As I finished my decadelong quest to write this book, in March 2010, Sherwood Schwartz finally managed to package the *Gilligan's Island* feature film project. As of May 2011, the burning questions are still unanswered: Who will play Gilligan? Will the new Professor be able to fix a hole in the boat? The attachment people of my age have to this material is remarkable. The burden on fresh actors to embody the castaways will be heavy. I cannot predict what sort of movie *Gilligan's Island* will make in the second decade of the twenty-first century. Will it be clever and transformative, like *The Brady Bunch Movie* (Betty Thomas, 1995) or *Star Trek: The Wrath of Khan* (Nicholas Meyer, 1982), or will it be ham-fisted and bizarre, like *The Honeymooners* (John Schultz, 2005) or *The Dukes of Hazzard* (Jay Chandrasekhar, 2005)?

The hope that the *Gilligan's Island* movie can be witty and successful is surely justified. Schwartz's other show, *The Brady Bunch,* provided screenwriters the opportunity to return to and camp up the 1970s. But, more to the point of the argument of this book, *Star Trek: The Wrath of Khan* shares with its *Star Trek* television series source and *Gilligan's Island* an inclination to mine the great ideas and culture of Western civilization. The 1982 film uses references to Charles Dickens and Herman Melville to return to its original source text, a show obsessed with William Shakespeare. While Schwartz turns *Hamlet* into a musical, Gene Roddenberry and his writers convert Captain Kirk (William Shatner) into Petruchio from *The Taming of the Shrew* (1594) in "Elaan of Troyius" (season 3, episode 69, December 20, 1968). Indeed, one would come close to rehearsing *Macbeth* (1607) by reciting *Star Trek* episodes "Dagger of the Mind" (season 1, episode 9, November 3, 1966) and "All Our Yesterdays" (season 3, episode 79, March 14, 1969) as the prime examples. As I have hoped to demonstrate in this book, *Gilligan's Island,* like its fellow traveler, *Star Trek,* is a fertile ground for building utopianism out of the great literature of Western civilization.

But it is not just the smart referencing that distinguishes *Gilligan's Island.* As I have demonstrated, the performativity in the show is its key. Unlike *Star Trek,* yet like the plays of Samuel Beckett, the show strips the medium to its bare essentials. All Beckett needs to develop character and theme is a bare stage with Vladimir and Estragon standing on it. All Schwartz needs to discuss the central importance of human beings' basic performative social nature is Gilligan and a phony lagoon in the middle of Los Angeles. That other sitcoms felt the need to blatantly belabor their roots in performativity—from *I Love Lucy* through *Seinfeld*—but that *Gilligan's Island* did not, makes Schwartz's show the most surprising TV milestone of all.

WORKS CITED

Alvey, Mark T. "The Absurd Situation Comedy of the 1960s: A Method 105
    and Meaning to Its Madness." MA thesis. U of Texas at Austin, 1985.
Bakhtin, Mikhail. *Rabelais and His World*. Bloomington: Indiana UP, 1984.
Barker, David. "Television Production Techniques as Communication."
    Critical Studies in Mass Communication 2 (1985): 234–46.
Bathroom Reader's Institute Staff. *Uncle John's Bathroom Reader*. New York:
    St. Martin's, 1998.
Bazin, André. *What Is Cinema?* Vol. 1. Berkeley: U of California P, 1968.
Beckett, Samuel. *Endgame and Act without Words*. New York: Grove, 1958.
———. *Krapp's Last Tape and Other Dramatic Pieces*. New York: Grove,
    2009.
———. *Waiting for Godot: A Tragicomedy in Two Acts*. New York: Grove,
    1954.
Burt, Richard. *Unspeakable ShaXXXspeares: Queer Theory and American
    Kiddie Culture*. New York: St. Martin's, 1998.
Butler, Judith. *Excitable Speech: A Politics of the Performative*. New York:
    Routledge, 1997.
———. *Gender Trouble: Feminism and the Subversion of Identity*. New York:
    Routledge, 1990.
Camus, Albert. *The Myth of Sisyphus and Other Essays*. New York: Vintage,
    1991.
Cantor, Paul A. *Gilligan Unbound: Pop Culture in the Age of Globalization*.
    Lanham, MD: Rowman, 2001.
———. *Shakespeare: Hamlet*. Cambridge: Cambridge UP, 1989.

Castleman, Harry, and Walter J. Podrazik. *Watching TV: Four Decades of American Television.* New York: McGraw, 1982.

De Lorde, André. *Au Téléphone.* 1902. *Gaslight.* 28 July 2010. http://gas light.mtroyal.ca/atteleph.htm.

Dixon, Wheeler Winston. *Disaster and Memory: Celebrity Culture and the Crisis of Hollywood Cinema.* New York: Columbia UP, 1999.

Foucault, Michel. "What Is an Author?" *Textual Strategies: Perspectives in Post-Structural Criticism.* Ed. Josue V. Harari. Ithaca, NY: Cornell UP, 1979. 100–120.

Frye, Northrop. "The Argument of Comedy." *English Institute Essays, 1948.* Ed. D. A. Robertson Jr. New York: Columbia UP, 1949. 58–73.

Gallagher, Scott Michael. *Geneva.* New York: Publish America, 2007.

Goffman, Erving. *The Presentation of Self in Everyday Life.* New York: Doubleday, 1959.

Goodall, Jane R. *Performance and Evolution in the Age of Darwin: Out of the Natural Order.* London: Routledge, 2002.

Green, Joey. *The Unofficial Gilligan's Island Handbook.* Los Angeles: Warner, 1988.

Grossman, Andrew. "The Smiling Cobra [Profile of James Aubrey]." *Variety Life* June/July 2004: 68–78.

Kearney, Mary Celeste, and James Moran. "Ida Lupino." *The Encyclopedia of Television.* Ed. Horace Newcomb. Chicago: Museum of Broadcast Communications, 2004. 1389–391.

Lewis, R. W. B. *The American Adam.* Chicago: U of Chicago P, 1959.

Marc, David. *Demographic Vistas: Television in American Culture.* Rev. ed. Philadelphia: U of Pennsylvania P, 1996.

Marx, Leo. *The Machine in the Garden: Technology and the Pastoral Ideal in America.* Cambridge: MIT P, 1964.

Melville, Herman. *Moby-Dick; or, The Whale.* Northwestern-Newberry ed. Vol. 6 of *The Writings of Herman Melville.* Evanston, IL: Northwestern UP, 1988.

Minow, Newton. "The Vast Wasteland." *Equal Time: The Private Broadcaster and the Public Interest.* Ed. Lawrence Laurent. New York: Atheneum, 1964. 45–69.

Mittell, Jason. "The Value of *Lost,* Part Two." *Flow: An Online Journal of Television Studies.* 18 Sept. 2005. http://flowtv.org/2005/08/the-value-of-lost-part-two/.

Morowitz, Laura. "From Gauguin to *Gilligan's Island.*" *Critiquing the Sitcom: A Reader.* Ed. Joanne Morreale. Syracuse: Syracuse UP, 2003. 116–28.

Noddings, Nel. *Caring: A Feminine Approach to Ethics and Moral Education.* 2nd ed. Berkeley: U of California P, 2003.

O'Leary, John, and Rick Worland. "Against the Organization Man: *The Andy Griffith Show* and the Small-Town Family Ideal." *The Sitcom Reader: America Viewed and Skewed.* Ed. Mary M. Dalton and Laura R. Linder. Albany: State U of New York P, 2005. 73–84.

Rabelais, François. *Gargantua and Pantagruel.* New York: Penguin, 2006.

Rowe, Kathleen. *The Unruly Woman: Gender and the Genres of Laughter.* Austin: U of Texas P, 1995.

Sarris, Andrew. *The American Cinema: Directors and Directions, 1929–1968.* 1968. New York: Da Capo, 1996.

Schatz, Thomas. *The Genius of the System: Hollywood Filmmaking in the Studio Era.* Minneapolis: U of Minnesota P, 2010.

Schirato, Tony, and Susan Yell. *Communication and Culture: An Introduction.* London: Sage, 2000.

Schwartz, Sherwood. *Inside* Gilligan's Island: *A Three-Hour Tour through the Making of a Television Classic.* New York: St. Martin's, 1994.

Snow, C. P. *The Two Cultures.* 1959. Cambridge: Cambridge UP, 1993.

Spigel, Lynn. *TV by Design: Modern Art and the Rise of Network Television.* Chicago: U of Chicago P, 2008.

Stoddard, Sylvia. *TV Treasures: A Companion Guide to* Gilligan's Island. New York: St. Martin's, 1996.

Walton, Priscilla L. *Our Cannibals, Ourselves.* Urbana: U of Illinois P, 2004.

INDEX